Arizona's
Haunted
History

Jill Pascoe

IRONGATE PRESS
Gilbert, AZ

Photography by Jill Pascoe

Author photograph by Joshua Pascoe
Painted Desert photographs by James Goho

ISBN 978-0-9754746-1-7

Library of Congress Control Number: 2008927219

2nd Printing 2012

Published by:

IRONGATE PRESS
1237 W. Seascape Dr.
Gilbert, AZ 85233
http://irongatepress.com
info@irongatepress.com

Cover photograph of Vulture Mine
Back photograph of the Grand Canyon
Printed in Canada

Dedication

For Adam,
who was there for every step of the journey.

Table of Contents

Acknowledgements

T his undertaking would not have been possible without the support from the historic sites, museums, hotels and ghost towns featured in this book. I am most grateful to all who shared their stories with me: Myranda Symons of the Bisbee Grand Hotel; Jay and Joanne Gammons of Gammons Gulch Ghost Town; Stephanie, Joyce, Alan, and Sharon from Goldfield Ghost Town; Don Robertson and Gina Walker from Gold King Mine and Ghost Town; Rochelle Garcia of the Jerome Historical Society; Bert Elizabeth Ijams from the Prescott Fine Arts Association; John Holst of the Red Garter Inn and Bakery; Kathy Farretta of the Riordan Mansion; Don Garate of Tumacácori National Historic Park; Kris Anderson of Vulture Mine; and Jesse Torres of Yuma Territorial Prison. I would also like to thank everyone else who spoke to me off the record as their stories also helped to shape this book. Finally I would like to thank my family for their tireless editing help and Josh and Adam for all their patience and support through the creation of this book.

Introduction

Arizona's storied history brings many images to mind. Cowboys, highway robberies, soiled doves working in brothels, saloons, shoot-outs and all the images of the Wild West that have come to us through history books and movies. It is an environment of contrasts. The desert seems eons old. Yet its cities boast contemporary architecture, culture, and high tech industries. Arizona is the home of ancient indigenous cultures and civilizations with impressive monuments and was explored by the Spanish conquistadors. But its modern time was founded on the knowledge of the local tribes, the backs of hard working miners, the steel hands of tough lawmen, and by men and women daring enough to try their luck in an unforgiving landscape of ever-present danger. Many failed but many more succeeded and flourished through a wild history in the harsh desert; many also continue their daring exploits beyond the gates of death.

We often imagine the stories these old towns of Arizona and their old buildings have to tell. But when we visit these ghost towns, and walk the real streets of Tombstone, explore the ruins of the Tumacácori, search for the Lost Dutchman Mine, we can almost hear the spirits of the past talking to us. That low whispering is more than just a lonely wind from the desert. What is that dark shadow passing by us when there are no clouds in the blue sky? Even our hotel rooms may cause us to wonder if the light that just flickered off was done by unseen hands. For the history of Arizona is not just wild, it is also haunted.

In this collection of seventeen tales you will meet women, men, and children who still haunt the homes they inhabited long ago, the buildings in which they once worked, and the landscapes they explored. You will discover haunted hotels and inns around the state where you can spend a feverish night with a spirit. Visit some of the most beautiful state parks and National Monuments in Arizona and learn the history the sites have to offer, but also be aware that around the corner a mysterious shadow lurks. Walk the streets of ghost towns that have been recreated to give you an exact experience of what life was like when Arizona was just beginning and during its Wild West days. See the actual ghost towns of Arizona, where the remains of the buildings speak for themselves about their dark past, and where the shadowy spirits of former residents appear as well.

This book speaks about the ghosts within their historical, architectural, archaeological, and sometimes geological contexts. Arizona is rich in its wonders. Here you will find stories of Arizonans, who are so enraptured by its beauty they have returned from the grave.

You will experience all of this as you travel through

these pages. So pull up a chair to your fire, put the lights on low, and enjoy your journey through Arizona's haunted history.

Jerome Grand Hotel

I

Jerome
America's Largest Ghost Town

Perched precariously above the sweeping vista of the Verde Valley sits the ghost town of Jerome. Perhaps ghost town is not really accurate for this town, which has been reborn as an active artist's retreat and a trendy tourist destination. But in comparison to what it once was, Jerome has certainly dwindled in size, and the abandoned buildings and crumbling ruins throughout this former bustling mining town are grim reminders of its past. However, ghost town is a good name for another reason; Jerome seems to be a favorite haunt for many of its departed. Virtually every building teems with spirits, the streets are not safe from the dead, and ghosts even take over the playground swings. Here you may be dizzied not only by the heights but also by roaming lost souls, some of whom may be atoning for their wicked ways while alive.

When one visits Jerome today it seems amazing anyone would have built a town teetering on the side of Cleopatra Hill, with Mingus Mountain looming sinisterly in the background. The story of Jerome is forever linked with mining and because of what was found here the town was born, boomed, and eventually abandoned.

In 1876 the first mining claims were made in the Black Mountains of Jerome. In 1882 these claims would be combined as the United Verde Copper Company. A small smelter was built and it seemed that the town was taking off, being named Jerome in 1883; but in 1884 the smelter closed. William Clark took control of the United Verde Copper Company in 1888 and production in the mines resumed. The population of Jerome swelled and production in the mines was unprecedented. In 1894, 11 million pounds of copper containing 7.5 million ounces of silver and 1.5 million ounces of gold was mined. Jerome became known as the "Billion Dollar Copper Camp."

Integral to the boom in Jerome was the introduction of the railway to this region. The high cost of transportation caused the initial failure of the mine. In the early 20th century Jerome was the largest copper mine in Arizona. The town swelled to a population of over 15,000 people, crammed along the steep slopes of Cleopatra Hill. The streets curve and switch back on each other, slowly making the climb up the mountain. Houses and businesses cling perilously to the sides of the mountain. Several times in the early years of Jerome fires destroyed the town, principally in 1897, 1898, and 1899, after which citizens finally began to change the way they constructed buildings to prevent the spread of fires. Stone buildings replaced the former timber framed buildings on the main street and firewalls were built between businesses to help prevent the spread of fire.

Epidemics were also rampant in this mining town, with outbreaks of smallpox, scarlet fever, and influenza spreading rapidly through Jerome resulting in many deaths over the years. Some people believed that the fires and disease were just rewards for this mining town. By 1903 Jerome was known as the wickedest town in America, having surpassed the reputations of Deadwood and Tombstone. It was reported in the New York Sun in 1903 that perhaps Jerome needed one more fire to purify the town.

In 1912 James Douglas bought the Little Daisy Mine, and by 1916 Jerome boasted not one but two bonanza mines. The copper vein found at the Little Daisy was five feet thick making it the richest ever found in American mining. Sadly, the Great Depression drastically affected Jerome. When copper prices dramatically fell in 1929 and continued to decline for the next four years, production on the mines fell and the mines were completely closed in 1931. However, Jerome was the little town that could, and in 1935 the mines reopened. But tragedy would fall on this town once again when an entire block in the business section was destroyed. It is believed that a fault under the town of Jerome, along with high groundwater, mine blasts from the mine, and a possible seismic event caused these buildings to crumble and fall down the hill. Jerome's jail was one of the buildings affected. Today it can be seen well across the street from its original site, and despite steel barriers anchoring it in place, the jail is still sliding down the hill.

As elsewhere in Arizona, the mines in Jerome eventually dried out, and shut down for good in the early 1950s. The population dropped dramatically with Jerome becoming a virtual ghost town. The few citizens that remained worked to make it a tourist attraction, and in the 1970s it also became a haven for artists. Every year a reunion for former residents is held at Spook Hall (the former JC Penny building and largest gathering place) on the third weekend in October. Spook in this sense referring to Jerome as a ghost town, not the otherworldly residents that inhabit this town as well. There are so many ghost stories in Jerome that it is difficult to find a hotel, restaurant, or home without a story to tell. During our visit in October 2006 we stopped into a local wine bar, and as we entered the staff were talking about their resident ghost causing problems. I had not even asked about the ghosts; it seems otherworldly entities are just a common topic of conversation here.

I spoke with Rochelle Garcia of the Jerome Historical Society who has a wealth of knowledge regarding the local lore of haunted spots. Every year the Jerome Historical Society conducts a ghost walk around town in October. One of the stories they tell is the murder of Sammie Dean. She was a prostitute found strangled to death on the streets of Jerome on July 7, 1931. An inquest never found anyone responsible for her death. Many residents of Jerome see the misty form of Sammie Dean wandering the streets, and lingering around the house where she once lived, which is now a private residence near Spook Hall. As many people who work during the day in Jerome leave for the night, the streets become quiet and an eerie ambience settles across the town. That is when Sammie Dean walks the streets, doomed to meet her deadly lover all over again. No one knows how she met her destiny. Had she spurned the unwanted advances of a man lurking for her in a forgotten alley? Was it a miner with rock-hardened hands and full of anger from drink? And now, every night does she again meet her doom, eternally? There is a creepy stillness in Jerome at night and sometimes even the stars, often brilliant, seem to slip back away into the heavens. Something ominous hangs in the air. Your heart leaps at movement down the street. You may hear a faint plaintive cry like a pebble falling into a deep well. But then, maybe it is only the shadows playing their tricks and the mind making something out of silence.

Although strange encounters are commonplace in Jerome, they are not welcomed and always leave a sense of unease. Rochelle told me one that happened to her while walking through the Upper Park. There are three parks in Jerome, and stairs take you between the parks and the winding main street of town. Upper Park is on the way to the Historical Society's building, near the top of the town. While walking through this park Rochelle saw two of the four swings moving as if ghostly children were swinging in them. There was no wind at all (the flag was completely still) and the swings kept on swaying and did not slow down, as you would expect if someone had just jumped off and run away quickly. She found the experience very unnerving and quickly left. Oddly this happened another time; two of the four swings seemed to be moving of their own will; again there was no wind, the flag and trees were still. This time she stayed for several minutes and finally left, with the swings still moving on their own. With all the tragic fires and epidemics in Jerome many children died over the years. Perhaps here two young children come back to play, laughing and swinging for eternity.

Rochelle also told me a story about the Boyd Hotel. The Boyd Hotel was originally built in 1897, but burned down, and was replaced with a brick structure which stands today. The lower floors housed businesses and the top floors were used as a hotel and boarding house. Today the top floors are used as apartments, and the ground floor has three stores, including a pottery shop. The renovation of the ground floor occurred in the 1970s but the two upper floors were empty from the 1920s until their renovation in 2005.

One year before a ghost walk, Rochelle was in the building with another employee of the Historical Society. The top two floors were gutted at this time, and they were standing in this open space, when they heard a noise from outside the building but there was no one there. It was a sound they knew did not belong. What was it that made them uneasy and unsettled standing in the great open space? Later Rochelle and her companion discovered they were in the same area where the photographer F.M. Bremman had killed himself. Another time, a husband and wife were using the space to film some short stories about Jerome and for three straight nights the smoke alarm came on at 2:00 a.m. for no reason. When they stopped filming, the unusual activity with the smoke detectors ceased. Later, after the apartments were constructed, a tenant who was living in the area where the photographer killed himself reported bright lights in the dark like a camera flashing.

The Historical Society's building itself is the former Episcopal Church, and now houses a large archive. While this building does not appear to have any spirits, Rochelle has seen a shadow walk past the window of the building on a few occasions. This window is in the back of the building, and it is not possible for a person to walk back there. Perhaps this is just another of the many wandering lost souls of Jerome.

During our visit to Jerome we lunched at the Haunted Hamburger Restaurant, which considering its name seemed a likely spot for a haunting. While enjoying our meal, I asked the staff if there were any ghost stories about the building. I was told when the owners bought the place fourteen years ago they restored it, which took about four years. During the restoration hammers would always go missing. One day they opened up the attic, which had been sealed off, and found all of the hammers in one corner. They left them there, as an offering to the building's spirits and no more hammers went missing. It seems that since the restoration it has been quiet on the ghostly front at this restaurant, but it is still worth a visit for the food and the views of the Verde Valley.

Jerome is probably best known for its haunted hotels, and perhaps best known is the Jerome Grand Hotel, which sits high at the top of the town. A mile high, the views from this hotel of the Verde Valley, the town of Jerome, and the San Francisco Peaks are fabulous. Sunset is especially enchanting as the fading light paints the landscape in pinks, blues, and purples. This building was constructed as the United Verde Hospital in 1927 in the Spanish Mission style, and is the last major building to have been constructed in Jerome. The hospital was built to withstand the hundred thousand pounds of dynamite set off by the mine and to be fireproof. It is amazing that this five-story structure was built on a fifty-degree slope, a true engineering feat. The hospital closed down in 1950 when Jerome was abandoned after the mines closed. The building sat vacant until 1994 when it was bought by Larry Altherr, and the hospital was reborn as the Jerome Grand Hotel in 1996. Now this former hospital is a National Historic Landmark with priceless views.

The hotel is famous for its 1926 Otis elevator, the oldest original "self service" elevator in Arizona. It is a unique ride requiring a key to open the door and make the elevator move between floors. Since we stayed at the Jerome Grand just prior to Halloween, the entire hotel was decorated for the spooky holiday including the elevator. This elevator is reputed to have killed an orderly, Claude Harvey, in 1935 when he was crushed to death beneath the elevator. His death was ruled an accident, although rumors have circulated that it was in fact a murder. The murder theory should be considered since the elevator moves slowly and doesn't sit flat on the basement floor. Furthermore, for a malfunction to have occurred there would have had to be tampering with the safety switch. The elevator was found to be in perfect working order by an elevator technician at the time of the tragedy.

Regardless of how he died, Claude Harvey's spirit has returned and roams the halls and the boiler room of the Jerome Grand Hotel. The elevator can be heard moving when in fact it is parked on the top floor. While we were staying at the hotel the elevator came up to the third floor where we were staying, even though I didn't call for it (nor was there anyone else around). It just seems to move on its own sometimes, or perhaps Claude Harvey is reliving his last ride.

Many people believe the third floor is the most haunted location in the hotel, hearing voices when there is no one in sight, seeing lights flickering on and off with no apparent cause, and smelling cigar smoke in an empty hallway. Two female ghosts have been seen wandering the halls, one a nurse holding a clipboard, and the other a woman in white, supposedly a woman who died in childbirth. Rooms 31, 33 and 39A and 39B have been marked as particularly haunted. We stayed in 39A and 39B during our time at the Jerome Grand. It was a wonderfully spacious two-room suite and I did hear voices while in the rooms, but what they were saying was unclear. The conversation came through muffled and in whispers. However, this suite is right next to the stairwell, and voices may travel very easily through the hotel.

The Jerome Grand has a wonderful restaurant called the Asylum Restaurant, which is a hotspot of activity in the hotel. The ladies room is where the emergency room was originally, and shadowy forms have been seen here. While we did not eat at the restaurant (room service seemed more advisable with a toddler), I wandered the second floor extensively, which had been festively decorated for Halloween. I did not see anything unnerving during my visit at the Jerome Grand, but perhaps the spirits were avoiding me or shunning the make-believe of

Halloween, for they know the real story of the long night of the dead.

Other hotels that boast ghosts in Jerome include the Inn at Jerome, the Connor Hotel, and the Ghost City Inn. During your visit you can stay at any one of these fine hotels, or enjoy a drink at the Spirit Room in the Connor Hotel, where you just might encounter spirits of more than one kind.

Jerome is a city of ghosts. Even though this town almost became a ghost town, it now boasts itself as the mile high town with the fifty-mile view. Indeed the views from Jerome are breathtaking, and it is easy to understand why ghosts would not want to leave this town that is so high up in the sky.

Red Garter Inn

2

The Red Garter Inn Bed and Bakery
A Ghost Called Eve

Today in Williams, Arizona two hundred thousand tourists a year enjoy the Wild West shows and gunfights between the Cataract Creek Gang and Marshall John B. Goodmore, before climbing aboard historic trains and heading north to the Grand Canyon. Just across the train tracks, visitors can get another taste of Arizona history by staying at a restored saloon and bordello. The Red Garter Inn, located along historic Saloon Row, offers rooms with beautiful antiques and a wonderful bakery on the ground floor. However, it also offers something visitors might not be expecting, the ghost of one of the ladies of the night has never left her job and continues to visit men staying in her room.

Williams was first settled in 1876 and is named for the Bill Williams Mountain, which towers over the town. In the early 1800s fur trading extended into Arizona, and one of the greatest fur trappers was William Sherley Williams. Williams trapped all over the western states, but enjoyed retreating into the area that would eventually be named after him. The railroad first arrived in Williams in 1882, and the Sante Fe Railway connecting Williams to the Grand Canyon was completed in 1901. This railroad brought tourists to the South Rim of the Grand Canyon and Williams' reputation as the "Gateway to the Grand Canyon" began. During the early 1900s Williams was also known as a rough and rowdy frontier town with gambling houses, saloons, brothels, and opium dens.

In the 1920s, the famed Route 66 came through Williams, bringing tourists along with it. The saloons and brothels continued to operate during this period, despite prostitution being outlawed in Arizona in 1907. Throughout the state this law was loosely enforced, especially when the operation of these businesses was essential to the economy of a town, such as it was in Williams. These houses of ill repute lasted in Williams until the 1940s. In the 1950s Highway 40 was constructed, bypassing Williams, and it seemed like this once wild town would fade away into history. In 1984 the Williams historic business district, which includes the Red Garter Inn, was placed on the National Register of Historic Places. In 1989, the restored railcars of the Grand Canyon Railway operated once more, and today Williams is again the Gateway to the Grand Canyon. The three locomotives that are used from the Williams Depot date from 1906 to 1923, and all engines and cars have been painstakingly restored to give passengers the feeling that they have been transported back into the Wild West days of Arizona's history.

The Red Garter Inn was built in 1897 by August Tetzlaff, a German tailor. The building was designed specifically as a saloon and a brothel. The inn has upscale architectural features, more in keeping with a fine Victorian house of the period, including the Romanesque arch out front, oak beamed ceilings, and gleaming window and door trim complete with bullseye corner blocks and transoms over the doorways. The Red Garter was built to be a first class establishment. The upstairs of the building, which was the brothel, was designed to serve the clients and make money for the owner. The rooms were small at the back, but become larger towards the front; the room at the very front of the inn was the opulent showcase for the best gal. Originally there were eight cribs (rooms used by the girls and their customers). The top floor also included a parlor where the girls enjoyed their treasured leisure time. Today the former brothel houses four sumptuous guest rooms.

The saloon and brothel were completely separate businesses, with separate entrances in the front and the back of the building. There was also a two-story outhouse in the back. The bottom level served the saloon and the top served the girls and their clients.

The Red Garter Inn was built to serve a future need. With

the railroad coming to Williams and the silver and copper mines planned in the Grand Canyon, there would soon be the demand for such a place. However, things did not pan out. The mine folded in the Grand Canyon. The Red Garter Inn did operate as a saloon and a brothel, but it was not the high-end establishment envisioned when it was designed. The clients included cowboys, working class men, and later sawmill workers. Mining was not a big industry in this area, so the inn did not serve the more lucrative clientele of mine owners, or mine workers with money in their pockets to spend.

Prostitution was a common way of life for many women in the old West because they had few viable options. There were simply not many ways for an unmarried woman to survive, especially if she was uneducated or did not speak English. Virtually all she could do was domestic work or become a prostitute. Prostitution generally paid better than domestic work and the lifestyle, especially in an upscale "parlor house," may have seemed more exciting to many young women, so this is the path they decided to take.

Archaeological investigations behind the property by John Holst, the owner of the Red Garter Inn, have revealed physical evidence of the location's shady past. The Chinatown of Williams was in this area behind the Red Garter and an opium den operated on the excavated site. Today in the lobby of the Red Garter Inn, visitors can see opium bottles, morphine needles, beer bottles, shot glasses, and whiskey bottles from this period.

The building went through several hands in the early years and was finally owned by a character named Longino Mora. Mora, originally from New Mexico, lived a long and colorful life. There are several pictures in the bakery of the Inn of Mora from the 1930s when he was managing the saloon and brothel. At this point he was on his fifth wife and had his twenty-fifth child, Carmina. It was this youngest daughter Carmina who gave many of the photographs to the Red Garter Inn.

One of these photographs is very strange. It pictures Longino Mora and a young woman dressed in black and smiling, which was very unusual in older photographs. The woman in black is standing in front of an old buffet. There is also a mirror in the photograph and if you look carefully you can see the buffet in the mirror and the reflection of a sign the woman is standing next to, but she is not reflected in the mirror. John Holst comments that this woman does not look like the young woman who has been seen by some of his male visitors, but it is odd nonetheless. Was the Red Garter haunted as far back as the 1930s? Who is the woman in the photograph?

As a saloon and a brothel the Red Garter Inn saw some wild times through its years in business, and likely some violence as well. In fact local sheriffs received numerous reports through the years that somebody had been shot or killed in the building. They would do an intense investigation, including searching into the 100 foot deep outhouse behind the building, but they never found a body.

Holst comments, "I have not seen a newspaper account yet. But one of the accounts that I had from one of the local characters, was that he remembered vividly that someone was stabbed on the stairs, and that they died out front, and the indication was that maybe this was why the brothels along this street were closed in the mid 1940s. I don't have any proof of it, but it is one of those things that could well have happened here."

Speculation is if one of the men was stabbed on the stairs, then one of the gals from the brothel did it. Again, there is no proof that this occurred, but it is possible. Certainly if someone was stabbed upstairs, it was likely the work of one of the ladies of the house. Perhaps she was protecting herself from an unwanted lover or helping a friend who was being beaten by a client. The old days in the West were tough and women had to be equally tough to survive. Was this lady who was part of the stabbing Eve who haunts the Best Gal's Room of the inn? No one can be certain, but it is clear that one of the gals from the brothel has never left her post, and still works at night until this day.

Holst first became aware that he was sharing his building with more than paying customers when he heard doors slam at night for no reason. Literally dozens of times he would be upstairs and hear what sounded like a door slam. Every time he went downstairs to check and make sure all the doors were secure, they always were. No one was ever downstairs and there was never any explanation as to why the door would slam. To this

28

day guests report hearing doors slam, usually around midnight, and there is never an explanation for what has occurred. No earthly explanation at any rate. Perhaps it is the sound of the men entering and leaving the cribs, echoing down through the years. It's as if the ghosts of those cowboys, working class men, and sawmill workers are still looking for love at the inn.

The most common experiences occur in the Best Gal's Room. This is the suite that is at the front of the Bed and Bakery and it would have featured the most beautiful ladies of the house. It seems that one of these ladies, Eve, has never left. Indeed, Eve likes to show herself to male guests. She is reported as being a young Hispanic girl, with long dark hair. She wears a light negligee or nightgown, and exudes just enough of a glow to make her stand out. She is always seen with her hands in front of her cupped together, like she is holding something or asking for something. Whatever she is holding in her hands is not visible to those who have seen her and the meaning behind what she is holding, or asking for remains unknown.

Holst has stories as far back as 1996 when a woman came and told him that she was awake in bed and her husband was asleep, and then all of sudden the bed started to go up and down. Holst thought she was just making a joke about the old brothel. But since that time, around six people a year will come down and describe their experiences in the Best Gal's Room. Women typically mention feeling as if a kid was pushing the bed, or somebody was sitting on the end of their bed, or someone was brushing their arm very softly. It is always very gentle, to get their attention, but without trying to scare them. The male guests on the other hand generally see the lady Eve, and over the years, they have also heard the name Eve, echoing through the room, associated with the vision. For the most part she is seen in the front of the building, at the end of the bed, in the hallway, or floating through the sitting room.

There are also disturbances at the Red Garter Inn on the stairs. It is unknown if these are the result of Eve, or perhaps because of the stabbing that supposedly took place there. Holst has heard noises on the stairs, and guests have reported on it throughout the years. These disturbances often affect the motion sensor lights. The lights are controlled by a motion detector and should only come on if someone is going up or down the stairs. Strangely, through the years they will turn on by themselves when no one is walking on the stairs. This occurrence was so frequent that Holst thought the parts were defective, so he replaced all the parts, but it still occurs. Could this be the ghost of the client who was murdered on the stairs, could it be the ghost of a regular, coming back to visit his best gal for eternity, or could it be the best gal herself, as she wanders aimlessly through the building? Guests often comment on the ghosts. I looked at the notes in the Guest Book from the days prior to my visit and there were several about the ghosts. Two that caught my attention were "Enjoyed the night, even the singing ghost on the stairs," and "Enjoyed the best gal in the Best Gal's Room."

The brothel is not the only haunted area of the inn. The bakery has seen its share of unexplained occurrences as well.

The door slamming in the night has already been discussed, as well as the phantom in the old photograph. In the back left hand corner of the Bakery near a large table, there have been many reports of cold spots through the years. Visitors and ghost hunters have also seen a child hiding in the corner. But as quickly as the child is seen, it is gone again. Just beyond the table is a wall, with some built-in windows, and people have seen a shadowy face looking in through the window.

As with many haunted locations, peculiar things seem to happen frequently at the Red Garter Inn. There are problems with electrical appliances, televisions will turn on by themselves, items will go missing and then reappear, and objects will move slightly by themselves.

If you are planning a trip by rail to the Grand Canyon,

it would be worthwhile to spend the night at the Red Garter Inn Bed and Bakery. You can enjoy the gleaming antique furnishings, the wonderful woodwork and oak-beamed ceilings, a delicious freshly baked breakfast, and maybe, if you are lucky, you will have a personal encounter with a friendly ghost.

The Red Garter Inn is not the only location in Williams troubled by ghosts. This small town's historic downtown is so haunted that it boasts its own ghost tour. There are reports of ghostly activity at the Grand Canyon Hotel, Rod's Steak House, and the Williams Depot. Be sure to check out these haunted locations while visiting the Red Garter Inn and take the Saloon Row Ghost Tour. For tourists, there are plenty of ghosts to go around in Williams.

3

The Riordan Mansion and other Flagstaff Haunts
A Ghostly Past

Flagstaff is often referred to as the city of the Seven Wonders. Set in the Coconino National Forest, Flagstaff is surrounded by the Grand Canyon, Walnut Canyon, Oak Creek Canyon, Wupatki National Monument, Sunset Crater National Monument, and the beautiful and majestic San Francisco Peaks. Snuggled into this charming town is the Riordan Mansion, a fantastic Arts and Crafts style duplex that over the years may have housed more than just members of the Riordan family; ghosts have made this their home as well.

The Riordan brothers, Timothy and Michael, moved

near Flagstaff in the mid-1880s. Tim married Caroline Metz in 1889 and they were anticipating the arrival of their first child in the spring of 1890. That year, when Caroline's younger sister Elizabeth came to visit, Tim's younger brother Michael was sent to greet her at the train station. Destiny placed the two together, and love at first sight led to their marriage in 1892. The two young couples, of brothers and sisters, were so close to each other that they lived right next door.

Timothy and Michael's older brother Matt was the general manager of the Ayer Lumber Company in Flagstaff, the largest lumber mill in the region. Matt Riordan eventually purchased the lumber mill incorporating the Arizona Lumber and Timber Company. By 1897, Matt had many other interests and he sold out his shares in the company to his two younger brothers and their business partner Fred Sisson. The Riordan brothers became the largest employer in Flagstaff and were very involved with their community. They were responsible for bringing electricity to Flagstaff, supporting public schools, were instrumental in building a Catholic Church, and established the first library in town. As their prominence in the community grew, as well as their own families, the Riordan brothers needed larger, more modern homes.

Charles F. Whittlesey, who was in the Northern Arizona area designing the El Tovar Hotel at the Grand Canyon, was chosen to design the homes for the brothers. Whittlesey was a young architect educated in Chicago, influenced by the new American Arts and Crafts movement. This architectural style makes use of elements from the natural environment and was a strong movement away from the more ornate and fussy Victorian architecture that preceded it. The Arts and Crafts movement was most prominently displayed in bungalows for the middle class. The Riordan Mansion is a fine example of this housing style on a grand scale.

While the structure of the Riordan Mansion is a frame design, the local ponderosa pine log slab siding makes it look like a huge log house. Arts and Crafts houses use local building materials and stonework was very common. This was adapted at the Riordan Mansion by using local volcanic rocks at the base of the house, in the chimneys, and at the front arches of the house. The Arts and Craft style is known for its wonderful use of built-ins throughout the home and the Riordan Mansion is no exception. The libraries and living rooms have wonderful built-in bookshelves and cupboards. Window seats are nestled into the dining rooms and huge indoor swings were once suspended from the ceiling in the living rooms (one of these swings remains today). Wooden light fixtures, skylights and stunning blue and green stained-glass windows throw gleaming light into the matching dining rooms. For the Riordan Mansion is not one house, but two mirror homes, joined together by a thousand square foot common room, which houses a billiard table for both families to enjoy. The total square footage of the home is thirteen thousand square feet and it has all the modern conveniences available at the time. Hot and cold running water, central heat, electric lights, and a telephone were a few of the features that the Riordan families enjoyed when the house was completed in 1904. With a total of forty rooms it truly is an amazing house.

Since the Riordan Mansion remained in family hands until it became a state historic park, first opening to the public in 1983, there are numerous family records and all the furniture and textiles in the house are original to the family. There is an impressive collection of Arts and Crafts style furniture, including twenty pieces by Gustav Stickley and five pieces of Harvey Ellis's inlaid furniture. Gustav Stickley was the leading spokesperson for the Arts and Crafts movement in America, and a furniture maker and architect. He founded the periodical *The Craftsman*, and worked with Harvey Ellis to design house plans for the magazine. Ellis also designed furniture for Stickley. Stickley's designs, which embraced the Arts and Crafts movement, had a strong influence on Frank Lloyd Wright. The Riordan Mansion is a house where you feel you have been transported back in time, and can imagine yourself eating in the dining room or relaxing on the unusual indoor swing in the living room.

While all seems quiet at the Riordan Mansion, several events in the past hint that all is not quite as it appears with this house. Over the years there have been stories of ghosts.

The Riordan family was deeply religious and in the East Wing of the house you can see the small chapel on the stair landing. Caroline insisted that an electric light always be on at this landing in front of a statue of Christ. One day in 1943 when

Caroline was away in Los Angeles a maid passed by the landing and saw the light had gone out. She was going to change the light bulb, but the light flickered back on. No more thought was given to this strange event until a call was received that night. Caroline had died at the exact moment when the light on the stairs flickered off and back on. Was this Caroline's way of saying goodbye to her beloved house? If so it seems that she made peace, as this has been her only reported contact with her former home since her death.

Michael and Elizabeth's son Arthur had a visit from the other realm. In the 1910s he was alone one day in the West Wing when he heard balls on the billiard table, which was in the common room of the mansion. Assuming his cousins were playing a game, Arthur decided to join them, only to find the large room empty and balls still rolling. He was confused, but assumed someone had just left the room, only to discover that the entire East Wing of the house was empty at the time. Who was this mysterious billiard player who chose to visit him that day? Tragically Arthur and his cousin Anna both died of Polio on the same day in 1927. Neither of their ghostly forms has been seen through the halls of either wings of the house.

The final ghostly experience at the house is the mysterious pipe smoker. Blanche Riordan, Arthur's sister, was the last Riordan to live in the home, doing so until she passed away in 1985. Blanche enjoyed telling stories of the ghostly experiences that had occurred in the house, including the flickering light and the mysterious billiard player. In the East Wing of the house the family would smell pipe smoke every now and then. My guide, park ranger Kathy Farretta, admitted that she had once smelled pipe smoke in the East Wing, but was quick to give an explanation other than ghosts. She explained that old wood often just smells like pipe smoke. Is the mysterious pipe smoker just a scent of old wood, or is it perhaps Timothy Riordan walking through his former home, admiring the fine craftsmanship, and pleased to see future generations visiting his home?

Top photo courtesy of Riordan Mansion State Historic Park c. 1910

The echoes of the Riordan family can be felt throughout the mansion as furnishings, books, clothing, and paper records still remain of this proud family. Some visitors claim that they can feel the presence of the family in the rooms and halls. Perhaps they have just been taken back in time by the beauty of the home and how timeless it feels, or maybe they truly have been touched by someone from the past who is trapped, unable to move on.

If you would like to hear these ghost stories first hand in the home in which they occurred, be sure to attend the annual Halloween tours of the Riordan Mansion.

If having an up close and personal encounter with a spirit is on your vacation plans you do not need to leave Flagstaff. You can choose to stay at the famous Hotel Monte Vista or the Weatherford Hotel. Both hotels are reputed to be home to ghosts.

The Hotel Monte Vista is known to be particularly active, with ten different accounts listed on their website alone. This historic hotel, opened in 1927, became the place to stay for Hollywood's elite during the 1940s and 1950s. The Monte V was known for the best and friendliest service in town. In fact the service was so remarkable, that President Harry Truman had the hotel's barber flown to Phoenix because he wanted the best, and he knew he could get the best from the Hotel Monte Vista.

The most haunted rooms are supposed to be 210, 220, 305 and 306. We stayed at the Hotel Monte Vista during our time in Flagstaff, across the hall from 305 where a rocking chair is supposed to rock by itself. There was one odd occurrence in our room. When we first checked into our suite, I checked all the doors, to see where they led, and noticed a door in the back room, and was curious if it was another entrance to the hallway of the hotel. It was a closet door, and not needing it, I closed it. About an hour later I was again in the back bedroom, setting up my son's bed for the night, when I noticed a coat hanger on the outside doorknob of the closet door. I was certain this had not been there earlier when I checked the door, as it would have made it difficult for me to open the narrow door and look inside. No one else was in the room during this interval. Perhaps this was the spirit of a former maid offering help to ease our settling into the room.

The appearance of a phantom bellboy is the most reported ghost in the hotel. Hotel guests staying in Room 210 hear a muffled voice say "room service", but when they open the door there is never anyone there. The most famous hotel guest to experience this ghost was the actor John Wayne, who said the ghost seemed friendly, and he did not feel that his presence was threatening in anyway. I ventured down to the second story a few times during our two-night stay but did not see or hear anything unusual.

Another strange phenomenon that occurs at the Hotel Monte Vista is the sound of a baby crying in the basement. This crying is not heard by hotel visitors, but by hotel laundry and maintenance staff members. Those who experience the ghostly cries of this infant are so disturbed by the encounter that they often run terrified out of the basement, trying desperately to escape the harrowing sound.

Public spaces in the hotel are also reported to be the home to spirits, so even if you are not a registered guest at the Monte V, you might have the chance to see a ghost or two. The Cocktail Lounge is home to a ghostly couple, whose dancing continues for eternity. The lounge is also home to a male ghost. Three men robbed a bank in 1970, and during their escape one of the men was shot by a bank guard. Despite this injury, the men decided they should stop by the Hotel Monte Vista to enjoy a celebratory drink, and during their time there, the injured robber bled to death. He is thought to be responsible for the ghostly voice that says "Good Morning" to patrons and staff, perhaps as penance for his misdeeds while living.

The Weatherford Hotel, just down the street from the Hotel Monte Vista, was built by John Weatherford and opened in 1900. Next door to the hotel, he constructed a theatre. When the original theatre, The Majestic, burnt down in 1915, Weatherford rebuilt it and called it the Orpheum. Today both the Weatherford Hotel and Orpheum Theatre are reputed to be haunted.

The Weatherford Hotel

The most famous haunted spot in the Weatherford Hotel is the Zane Grey Ballroom. A beautiful woman is seen floating about the room, forever reliving an evening of dancing. Voices and whispers are heard near the bar. Are these patrons from the past enjoying a party for eternity? Other ghosts who are reported to haunt this hotel are a honeymoon couple who, legend says, were murdered in their hotel room, number 54. While this room has since been turned into a storage closet, staff and guests still report their presence in the hotel. The presence of this couple makes itself known in several ways, especially to the staff of the hotel. The couple has been spotted several times entering their former room. Staff hear their names being called out by an otherworldly voice on the fourth floor. And while walking down the hall staff report feeling a presence following them.

The Orpheum Theatre has had its share of ghostly encounters as well. Most activity seems to be in the bathrooms and concession area. Unusual activity includes toilets flushing by themselves and faucets running at full blast by unseen hands. Numerous employees and patrons have reported the sense of a presence in the men's restroom. A janitor saw a dark shadowy figure float through the aisles in the balcony well after the theatre had closed, and guests and staff had left for the evening. One night an odd occurrence unnerved the three staff members working the concession stand. As they stood and watched in amazement a roll of paper towels quickly unraveled, spilling onto the ground. One staff member bravely put his hand up to stop the rapidly rolling paper, and was successful until he pulled his hand away, and it began to roll once again.

Flagstaff is a beautiful mountainside town, with wonderful views and good clean air. The temperatures are a welcome break from the heat that permeates much of Arizona throughout the year. For a trip back in time, the Riordan Mansion is a true must. You might just be lucky enough to catch the rich deep scent of pipe tobacco in the air or hear a phantom billiard ball roll softly on the felt tabletop until it gently ricochets off another phantom ball. While in town stay at one of the haunted hotels, and maybe you will have a visit from the other side.

4

Painted Desert Inn
A Lonely Sentinel

Sweeping vistas of glorious colors engulf you when you visit the Painted Desert Inn. High on a cliff overlooking the Painted Desert, the inn seems like a lonely outpost in the Petrified Forest National Park. In the distance eerie traces of dry rivers meander forlornly through the desert, surrounded by vivid cliffs. There is little in the way of vegetation here and it is hard to imagine anything living among these hard rocks which dance and glint in the light. However, a solitary spirit continues to haunt the Painted Desert Inn, unaware that she has moved on, unable to let go of her view of such a stunning landscape.

The Painted Desert is in northeastern Arizona and is now a part of the Petrified Forest National Park. Here sedimentary rocks compressed together to create the Chinle Formation, a combination of mudstone, limestone, siltstone, and clay stone, which were deposited over two hundred and twenty million years ago. Through the years the layers have become compressed and eroded, and now display subtle bands of pastel colors, mainly pink and red, although blue, gray, brown, and white can be seen as well.

Although the landscape is glorious, the inn is a jewel in the setting. From a distant lookout, the Inn radiates a sandy, warm red glow. And it is almost a miracle that it is still standing as the inn has a history of narrow escapes from destruction.

Perhaps the building has a guardian angel. In 1953 it was damaged by fire and the manager died as a result of the fire. Several other times it was abandoned and left empty for years. A ranger said that before the latest restoration, the inn was shunned as there was a sense of terror surrounding it. People were afraid, felt chilled and sensed an uneasy presence around the inn. Stories speak about teenagers coming at night to smoke near the inn, before it was restored, and listen for spirits. It was for the thrill but some may have experienced more than they wished. Overlooking the dark desert bowl, cigarettes glowing crimson in the night, sometimes they would hear a wind rattle up out of the canyon. At first they would joke and laugh until something brushed their faces with a touch of bone followed by a strange wailing. Suddenly it turned cold and the wind flowed like tears on their faces. With the wind came a shadow. Then the cigarettes would be pulled from their freezing fingers and they would flee, leaving behind only a soft sad weeping.

The story of the Painted Desert and Petrified Forest National Park began millions of years ago during the Triassic period when the super continent Pangea began to drift apart. Then northeastern Arizona was seventeen hundred miles further south (and closer to the equator) than it is today. Unlike the desert climate that exists today, Arizona 225 million years ago was a tropical climate with a volcanic mountain range to the South called the Mogollon Highlands. Streams passed through the area and trees and logs washed down from these highlands and deposited themselves in mud and marshy lagoons. Over the years layers of sediment were deposited over these logs causing them to petrify. For millions of years this accumulation of sediment and periodic erosion continued, giving us the Chinle Formation that we see today. Also during this process the trees, logs, and animals that were trapped and buried under layers of sediment were petrified, that is literally turned into stone. While the logs that we see today in the Petrified Forest retain the exterior look of tree stumps and logs, their internal structure is much different with the organic matter having been replaced by minerals. We are looking at the same trees that were once looked at by dinosaurs.

In addition to the bands of sediment and color in the Painted Desert and the forest of petrified trees (none of which stand but rather lay strewn on the ground), there are also ancient ruins of the first people to live here. Several hundred years ago the Navajo moved into Arizona and found ruined pueblos. They called the people who had occupied them Anasazi, which means "enemy ancestors" or "ancient ones." The Anasazi (or Ancient Puebloans, as they are increasingly called) were not ancestors of the Navajo themselves.

When Arizona became a part of the United States in 1848 after the end of the Mexican War, surveyors began to explore their new territory. Starting in 1849 several topographical engineers noted the Petrified Forest, but it was not until 1853, when Congress wanted extensive topographical surveys in order to plan railroad routes, that an extensive survey was undertaken in this region. Leadership of this survey was under Lieutenant

Amiel Weeks Whipple of the Topographical Engineers, joining him was Heinrich Baldwin Mollhausen as an artist and topographer. This report and its illustrations gave an idea of what this unknown land was like. The outbreak of the Civil War stopped any further exploration of the area and the railroad was not laid down until the 1880s. Small towns popped up along the railway lines, and with this increase in population the forest of petrified trees became better known. When General Sherman came through the area in 1878 he asked for two specimens of petrified wood for the Smithsonian. This increased public knowledge of the area, but it was still such an isolated area that few tourists visited.

By the end of the nineteenth century the Petrified Forest was easily accessible by rail, and tours were being given. But while the views of the Painted Desert are beautiful and the petrified logs are unusual, the area did not have the monumental scenery found at Yellowstone or the Grand Canyon.

In 1906, under the Antiquities Act, the Petrified Forest was named a National Monument. While this designation was important in recognizing the significance of the site, it did not in reality offer any real protection for the Forest. The boundaries that were protected were limited in size, and no money was set aside for administering the new National Monument. From 1929 to 1940 the area flourished thanks to money and labor provided by Roosevelt's New Deal program, however the area protected was still limited and did not include the Painted Desert, or the Painted Desert Inn. It would not be until March 1958 that the

Petrified Forest became a National Park, and finally included the Painted Desert in 1962.

The Painted Desert Inn, itself a National Historic Landmark, was built in 1920 of local stone and petrified wood. It commanded a perfect view of the landscape of the Painted Desert. This small inn, known as the Stone Tree House, provided a place to stay in the remote and isolated desert, a place for a meal, or to purchase a souvenir.

In 1935 the Petrified Forest National Monument purchased the Stone Tree House. After their purchase of the inn, National Park Service architect Lyle Bennett redesigned the inn to reflect the movement towards the Rustic style of architecture, and to address some structural problems the inn was experiencing. The inn was redesigned in the Pueblo Revival style, and the work completed by the Civilian Conservation Corps during the Depression years. A volunteer at the gift shop at the inn spoke about the work crews here in the thirties, living in a make-shift camp and sending most of their earnings home to families. The gift shop is warm and inviting with ponderosa pine beams and aspen roofing and a spectacular stained-glass ceiling window. With a faraway look in his eyes, the volunteer said he would like to speak with the ghosts but there was only silence.

The inn's redesign used many local materials including ponderosa pine and aspen for the roof beams. Light fixtures in the inn were handmade from punched tin, skylight panels were hand-painted to reflect prehistoric designs, and the concrete floors were painted with designs based on Navajo blankets. With its new look the Painted Desert Inn reopened on July 4, 1940, and business was good for several years until the outbreak of World War II. With the decrease in travel business, the inn suffered and had to close in October 1942.

In 1947 the inn was updated yet again with the help of Mary Elizabeth Jane Colter, the architect and interior designer of the Fred Harvey Company. She created a new color scheme in the inn, and added windows to allow visitors to better enjoy the wonderful view. It was also at this time that the renowned Hopi artist, Fred Kabotie, was hired to paint murals on the dining and lunch room walls. The inn operated until 1963 when it was closed for many years due to structural damage, and in 1975 it was scheduled to be demolished. Public outcry saved the Painted Desert Inn, and it was reopened in 1976, and is open now as a museum. Time has not been kind to the Painted Desert Inn, years of neglect and the shifting foundation of the building (the inn was built on a seam of bentonite clay) has caused swelling and shrinking. Water damage has also occurred in the building, threatening the Kabotie murals. The inn was closed near the end of 2004 for rehabilitation and restoration. It reopened in May 2006 and today visitors can enjoy the beautiful murals and the views from this former Inn.

As mentioned earlier, in April 1953 tragedy hit the Painted Desert Inn when a fire broke out. Clinton Harkins, a park ranger, discovered the fire and ran into the building, breaking down the front door. He ran inside and found Mrs.

Marion Mace, manager of the inn, unconscious. He dragged her outside and then ran back into the historic inn and put out the flames with a fire extinguisher. When Harkins had successfully stopped the fire, he went outside only to discover that Mrs. Mace had died of smoke inhalation. The cause of the fire in the Painted Desert Inn that April night has not been determined, but as Mrs. Mace was a smoker, and the fire started in her bedroom, it seems likely that a cigarette left burning could be to blame. Whatever the cause it seems Mrs. Mace has not forgiven herself.

One day a visitor was walking outside on a trail by the inn, and heard a dry, thin voice say "there is a fire back there." He returned to the inn, and there was no fire. It is thought that this ghostly voice was Mrs. Mace reliving that tragic night. Another time when the building was closed a park ranger was walking outside and looked in through the windows of the inn and saw a figure pass by the window, walking from room to room. The ranger went into the inn, prepared to lecture a misplaced tourist, but found no one. She did however detect the faint acrid odor of cigarette smoke. Is this the remnants of Mrs. Mace revisiting her former home – the home she betrayed – the home she loved and cherished and now is she sentenced to patrol the Inn and keep it safe forever?

Before the most recent renovation the inn had the reputation of being a frightening place with strange noises occurring, especially on the ground floor. It was shunned because of this sense of terror. A ranger said people reported an uneasy presence and a brooding chill emanating from the inn. While some of this activity stopped after the restoration, there are still reports of floors creaking, alarms going off with no one visible to trigger them, and whispers in unoccupied rooms. Perhaps now that the inn has been restored to its former glory Mrs. Mace's ghost will be able to rest in peace, or perhaps this ghost, who met a tragic end, will always watch over this inn, forever enjoying the views, and making certain that no one else meets her fate.

The Painted Desert Inn

While visiting the Petrified Forest National Park and the Painted Desert take the time to visit the beautiful Painted Desert Inn. You might also want to walk the Painted Desert Rim Trail. It is unpaved but an easy walk along the rim. Below the rim there is the wondrous desert with its pastel bands of red, orange, pink and gray, where almost nothing grows. The rim itself is alight with the leaves and blossoms of juniper, cliffrose, and wild tea, which thrive in the volcanic soil. You will enjoy the views. At the inn, you will see history and maybe, just maybe, hear some faint footsteps and an echoing voice, while you catch the faint smell of cigarette smoke. While you experience the sights, smells, and sounds be comforted that you have been paid a brief visit from the other side. Relax and enjoy your visit and as you see the stunning views you will understand why this spirit does not want to leave.

5

Grand Canyon
Where Spirits Rise

It is one of the most beautiful natural wonders of the world. Every vista from the rim gives you a different perspective of the Canyon as the light bounces and reflects off the rocks. Down below, on the Colorado River, the Canyon towers above in shades of red, green, gray, and brown. It is eerily silent; at times the soft rush of the river is all you hear. In Grand Canyon Village tourists abound, but at certain times of the day you can find moments of solitude and quiet, with only the Canyon as your companion. This is the Grand Canyon, mysterious, beautiful, impossible to comprehend, and definitely haunted.

Only a few landscapes seem to evoke this feeling

of cosmic awe, this sense of the supernatural. The Grand Canyon is a very spiritual place and eons old. In canyon caves archaeologists have found split-twig figurines of mountain sheep and deer made by people who lived in this area four thousand years ago. About 1050, ancestral Puebloan people set up communities in arable lands in the canyon and on the rim. These Pueblo people are thought to be the ancestors of the Hopi people, who live in a region east of the Grand Canyon. Hopi people still return to honor a mineral spring. The Hopi believe all souls come from the Grand Canyon, and all must return here when they die, making it a place full of spirits and energy.

My travels took me to the Grand Canyon on a lovely weekend in November, with a stay booked at the famous El Tovar Hotel. Today five million people come and visit this, the Grandest of all the Canyons, every year. Options to get to the Canyon today include bus tours, cars, trains, and even by plane. But the Canyon was not always this accessible or so popular.

The Grand Canyon's history began two billion years ago when two titanic plates collided, creating rock layers that would be the foundation of the Canyon. Seventy million years ago the Rocky Mountains and Colorado Plateau began to form; the layers were now in place for the Grand Canyon to be carved. Around five million years ago the Colorado River flowed across the Colorado plateau, which over the millennia slowly eroded the soil, cutting down, and deepening the Canyon. Because some of the lower layers contained softer rock, they eroded faster and collapsed, creating the ridges and cliffs of the canyons.

While the area of the Grand Canyon has been inhabited by Native American Tribes for thousands of years, it was first discovered by Spanish explorers, led by García López de Cardenas, in 1540. At the time natural wonders held no importance; it was a barrier, a place to be avoided, and it would be another 236 years before another expedition made it to the Grand Canyon.

In 1776, Father Francisco Tomás Garcés was visiting the tribes along the Río Colorado, and encountered the Canyon, as it was the most direct route to the Hopi Villages he wanted to explore. He too saw nothing special in this Canyon, which he also viewed as a barrier.

The significance of the Grand Canyon changed in the 1800s with the 1848 Treaty of Guadalupe Hidalgo and the 1853 Gadsden Purchase which led to Arizona joining the United States. Exploration of the area increased as Mormon guides and colonists came from the North. From the East and South came traders and Army explorers. In 1869 John Wesley Powell led an expedition through the Grand Canyon, riding the rapids, and setting the foundation for further exploration. Tourists began to come to the Canyon and hotels began to open, including the Grand View Hotel in 1897.

The last one hundred years has seen a focus on the preservation of the Canyon. In 1906 the Act for the Preservation of American Antiquities was created and in 1908 the Grand Canyon was declared a National Monument by President Theodore Roosevelt. In 1919 The Grand Canyon became a

National Park, and the current park boundaries were established in 1975. In 1979 the Grand Canyon was named a World Heritage Site, and it is known as one of the Seven Natural Wonders of the World.

Today most visitors arrive at the Grand Canyon at the South Rim. The North and South Rim are only 10 miles apart, but it is a 215 mile car ride. The Canyon is 280 miles long and one mile deep covering a total of 1900 square miles. From the South Rim, visitors can walk the rim trail, drive between viewpoints, or take shuttle buses around the viewpoints. Grand Canyon Village offers exceptional views of the Canyon, the Grand Canyon Railway station, dining and shopping opportunities abound, and you just might see a ghost.

In 1901 rail service came to the Grand Canyon making it much more accessible and greatly boosting tourism. In 1905 the El Tovar, the grandest hotel in the South Rim, opened with luxurious features like steam heat, electric lights, and indoor plumbing, costing an astonishing $250,000. In 1909 the train station at the Canyon was built just below the hotel making it a convenient stop for visitors. Right out front of the hotel is the best view of all, the Grand Canyon.

The El Tovar Hotel is an interesting mix of styles. In many ways it is a glorified log cabin, with the refinements of a European villa. The location of the El Tovar, just twenty feet from the Canyon Rim, is supreme, although despite being built with 100 guest rooms (today there are 78 rooms), only three suites actually have direct views of the Canyon. This was done intentionally by architect Charles Whittlesey. He wanted to encourage guests to get out of the hotel and view the Canyon from the Rim itself. The hotel, with its dark brown stain and varied rooflines, seems to melt into the Canyon, and does not distract from the landscape around it.

El Tovar Hotel

Originally the Fred Harvey Company operated the El Tovar Hotel. Fred Harvey was responsible for bringing high standards of hospitality and service to the American West. He operated lunchrooms along rail lines that offered travelers good quality food, at a reasonable price, with consistent service. This was something that previously did not exist on the perilous journey west. Young unmarried women who wanted a good job and a little adventure joined the Fred Harvey Company and became known as Harvey Girls, serving meals at his lunch

59

counters. He then expanded to the hotel business with the El Tovar becoming the crown jewel of the company. Fred Harvey died in 1901 before the hotel was completed, but his son Ford Harvey took control of the company. The El Tovar was opened and run with the same level of expertise as all the other Fred Harvey establishments. Today that level of service can still be experienced at the El Tovar Hotel, especially with a recent renovation of the guest rooms. Visitors might experience another amenity during their stay; they might meet one of the hotel ghosts.

During my stay at the El Tovar Hotel I was lucky enough to stay in the Charles Whittlesey Suite, which had a large bedroom, a sitting room, and a huge balcony. While not one of the three suites that overlook the Canyon (these have to be booked up to a year in advance) I could see the Canyon from the balcony, and the room was comfortable and quiet. It did not appear to be haunted, although the third floor suites are known to have activity, especially the View Suites.

While people are in the dining room they often hear sounds coming from the View Suites above. Most commonly, guests report the sounds of children bouncing up and down on the furniture and the floor when there are no children staying in those rooms. This happens about three times a year, and the desk clerk I spoke with had received such a complaint once.

The attic of the El Tovar is home to a ghostly tricycle, which can be seen going through the walls. Perhaps after playing in the View Suites the ghostly children enjoy going for a ride in the attic.

The most famous stories of the hotel involve the painting of Fred Harvey, which hangs in the lobby of the hotel, just at the foot of the Grand Staircase. It is a rather large oil painting of the founder of the Fred Harvey Company. It is said that at night the spirit of Fred Harvey will come out of the painting and walk through the lobby. Workers in the kitchen have also reported that they have seen his ghostly image float through. Perhaps since the hotel was completed after his death Fred Harvey wants to see how everything looks and make sure it still meets the high standards set by him. After all when he was alive Mr. Harvey was known to make unannounced inspections of his lunchrooms and hotels.

The El Tovar is not the only haunted location in Grand Canyon Village. Directly across the road, also facing the Grand Canyon, is Hopi House. Mary Colter designed this adobe building typical in architectural style to the Pueblo Buildings of the Hopi people. She was employed by the Fred Harvey Company and designed many buildings in the Southwest. The Hopi House opened in 1905 just a few weeks before the El Tovar Hotel. Originally the Hopi People lived and worked in the building, entertaining guests with dances on the north platform at night. Authentic Native American Crafts have been sold here since it opened its doors in 1905, and in 1987 the Hopi House was declared a National Historic Landmark. Today, visitors can enjoy viewing the Hopi House on two floors filled with Native American merchandise from baskets, to pottery, to rugs, to jewelry. But there is more than just crafts in this building; two ghosts inhabit the house as well.

The two ghosts are known as the "Brown Boys" (this phrase was used as a term of endearment by the worker I spoke with, but I am unsure how the Hopi would view this name) and are young Hopi children who like to play and cause havoc in the store. They play with the lights in the gallery, including turning lights on and off inside of display cases. The staff member I spoke with said the lights in one of the second floor cases went out one morning, and the huge heavy display case had to be moved out and opened up in order to turn it back on. The light had not burned out; it had been switched off on the inside.

Also on display on the second floor are many large sheep. They are close to life size and made of wool. One morning when this staff member came in all the sheep had been placed in a circle in the middle of the floor. Everything had been in its proper place the night before, and there was no evidence that anyone had entered the building during the night.

These children might also be responsible for playing with some jewelry. One day an employee had two bracelets and she put them away in a storage case. Later that day when she went to retrieve them, there was only one bracelet. Two employees looked everywhere for the missing bracelet, and they couldn't find it anywhere, which was upsetting as it was valuable. The next morning the bracelet was under one of the sheep on the second floor, near the cash register. They had carefully looked around this area the day before with no sign of the bracelet. It is believed to have been the work of the "Brown Boys," two friendly spirits just trying to have fun.

Visitors and staff also hear footsteps from the third story of the building when there is no one there. Originally the Manager's quarters, this area is now used for offices. Could this be the "Brown Boys"? Or is there another spirit at play on the third story of the house?

Hopi House

Across the parking lot from the El Tovar Hotel and Hopi House is Verkamp's Curios. This shop first opened in 1906, although John Verkamp began selling curios in a tent at the Grand Canyon in 1898. The main floor of this building is a large curio shop, and the second floor was the original living quarters of the Verkamp family. Today the main floor is still selling souvenirs to visitors of the Grand Canyon, with an approach of something for everyone, from high end Native American Crafts, to simple souvenirs. I found a cute chipmunk stuffed animal for my son, which was a big hit. Thankfully it did not attract a spirit back to my house.

Four generations of the Verkamp family have operated the store making it the oldest family owned and operated gift shop in all of America's National Parks. It also might be the most haunted.

At various times visitors and staff have seen deceased members of the Verkamp family wandering the building. One particular story relates to the second generation of the Verkamp family. This generation had five children. One day when the current manager arrived he found five oranges lined up on the stairs, one on each step going up to the living quarters upstairs. There had been no oranges the previous evening when he had locked up, and yet there they were in the morning. To make the story even more odd there were no oranges in the store, and none available at the Grand Canyon at all at the time. He later learned that each of the Verkamp's five children would get an orange for Christmas. This was a very special treat at the Grand Canyon in the 1950s. Who set out the oranges is not known, but they were real, and the staff later enjoyed them as their own special treat.

The Grand Canyon itself has many stories of ghosts. One of the stories originates on the North Rim and is about a woman named Jennifer. In the 1920s this woman's son and husband went hiking and fell to their deaths. So overtaken by grief, she later hung herself in the Grand Canyon Lodge at the North Rim. People say they see her all the time on the North Rim in a white robe with pink and blue flowers looking for her husband and son. She looks very normal, and will approach visitors and ask if they have seen her husband and son, as she wanders for eternity looking for them. This is the Grand Canyon's version of the La Llorona legend, the wailing woman forever looking for her lost family.

The Grand Canyon is no stranger to tragedy as well as beauty and mystery. In 1956 two commercial airplanes collided over the Grand Canyon, killing all 126 people on board both planes. The planes smashed into the side of Chuar Butte and Temple Butte, a very remote part of the park, and quite difficult to access. While camping in this area rangers have heard voices calling for help and have observed strange lights.

The Grand Canyon is on most people's must see lists. Grand Canyon Village boasts wonderful accommodations and dining with world-class views, as well as several buildings on the National Register of Historic Places. The wonder and the beauty of the Grand Canyon certainly make this a place that needs to be visited, and perhaps that is why several spirits have never left. Some are still enjoying the view, while others are trying to find their way home, and some have come here as their final resting place, so full of wonder, and life, and spirit.

Bordello at the Gold King Mine and Ghost Town

6

Gold King Mine and Ghost Town
A Recreated Town Conjures back the Dead

Gold King Mine and Ghost Town is only one mile south of Jerome, Arizona along a winding dirt road, but it feels much farther away. Little remains here from the former mining town of Haynes itself. However the town has been wonderfully recreated and you feel as if you are in a real mining camp. Reminders of the tough old southwest town are everywhere. And, if you watch and listen carefully, you might see town folk from long ago wandering the dusty streets or hear the frantic picking of miners still trapped deep in the mineshaft. Even though most of the buildings of Haynes became rubble and ruin, there seems to be a time shift here conjuring back long dead citizens.

Haynes, Arizona was founded by the Haynes Copper Mining Company which in 1890 excavated a twelve hundred foot deep shaft hoping to find copper. The company's disappointment in not striking copper was mollified by the discovery of rich gold deposits. The mines operated until 1914, and the town had a post office from 1908 until 1922. After the mines closed and many people left, Haynes became a suburb of Jerome and an illegal dump. When Jerome became a ghost town itself in 1953, Haynes really emptied out, and it was essentially a junkyard when Don Robertson purchased the property in the 1980s.

Don describes the history of Haynes, "This place has just been a ghost town for so long. The mine closed in 1915 and everybody just moved out quick. I am told the first guy who moved tore his house down real quick, and put all the boards on a truck, and hauled the boards with him. So that was monkey see monkey do after that. Everybody thought that was what you did, you know. Because they did not own the property under the house, they just rented that. So if they moved, the house was theirs if they took it. If they walked off and left it, it belonged to the property owner. That is why there wasn't that much here when I got here; just a site and I went from there. But it is neat. And I really needed an empty space to put my things in. And it wasn't exactly empty. It had been emptied out and picked clean, and then for forty years no one was out here, so it was kind of used as an illegal dump. Things too big to take to the dump, or they just didn't want to haul it to the dump, they brought it here. So there were car bodies and truck bodies, and then they would come out here, and shoot them full of holes, so there wasn't anything that could be saved. Stoves, water heaters, you name it, stuff they didn't want to haul to the dump."

So Don spent a great deal of time cleaning out the site and then restoring the original bordello that remained on the property. Today, a recreated ghost town exists for tourists. Visitors can see an authentic 19th century working sawmill. It was this sawmill that produced the lumber for Goldfield Ghost Town (Chapter 12) and Gammons Gulch (Chapter 14). There is an authentic 1901 blacksmith's shop. The dentist shop is a former house that was on the road between Gold King and Jerome. Over the mountain Don found a gas station being used as a private home; he moved it to Gold King, where he renovated it to its present state. The log cabins are from near Flagstaff. A few buildings were too high on the surrounding hills to be seen, so Don brought them closer to the town site. Otherwise he constructed the buildings using the lumber from his historic sawmill. Moreover, the town site houses a large collection of antique trucks. You can also visit the original mineshaft. A petting zoo is on site as well and my son was delighted to run around after the chickens in the town. Other remnants from the past might greet you as you explore the mine: the ghosts of a miner and a lady of the night.

When Don first arrived at Gold King before he bought the property, he camped out on the land, experiencing first-hand the high desert and desolate ruins. During the early days, before it was cleared and rebuilt, Don often heard strange noises arising from the vertical mineshaft. Don explains, "Some of the town kids, they are grown now, they would come out here and camp with us sometimes. We would hear these noises and they would ask what they were. And I would say, one thing they could be is the ghosts of some miners that died, that are picking, still picking, trying to get out." Many visitors today have seen a miner near this old mine shaft. He wears a blue shirt, dark blue pants, and suspenders. Sometimes his apparition is accompanied by creepy laughter. The miner has also been seen in the blacksmith shop; sometimes the branding irons in there will just swing back and forth on their own.

Gina Walker, who works at Gold King and lives on the site, has had encounters in her house. She told me, "One night at my house, which is just up the hill, my back door just kept opening and I could tell it was someone walking in who had a dog." In the middle of the night, when no one is around, she has heard noises as if a building is being constructed right beside her. Perhaps scenes replayed from the town's mining boom? At times a lantern in Gina's house will just swing back and forth on its own. She tries to stop it, and it will just start swinging again, sometimes for three days straight. It seems as if the Gold King Mine site is a residual haunting as the past recurs in sounds and sights.

The most frightening experience Gina had in her house occurred one night when she had a guest staying with her. Loud thundering noises woke her, as if a herd of javelina (wild pigs) was storming over her house. It was quiet for a heartbeat and then the same thundering noise from the side of the house. Upon investigation there was no trace of javelina or anything else to explain this horribly frightening sound. Only later did Gina learn that one year there was a very bad winter in the town, with heavy snow on the ground, and during an epidemic the only way the Doctor could reach Haynes was by the use of a team of dogs and a sled. Perhaps it was the echoes of the frantic Doctor rushing madly to his patients through the winter storm that Gina heard all these years later.

Gina is not the only one who has had personal experiences at home. Don is particularly haunted by the events of a night in

January 2006. While he acknowledges there have always been ghosts around the property, this was the first time one of them did anything bad to him. They threw him out of bed in the middle of the night. "That had never happened before and I have no idea what I did to piss them off. I got thrown out of bed, across the room. This arm was hit, I don't know what I hit, this arm here, and I cut my ear pretty bad. I just got up, got my gun, went around the house to see who the hell was here, who did it, and there was nobody there." Many uncanny things happen at this house. The washing machine turns itself on in the middle of the night; Don also hears the floorboards creak all the time in his house, "I will be sitting just watching TV, and I heard the boards squeak on the floor between me and the TV and I know there is a presence there."

Time is unclear in this ghost town. This was literally true at the gift shop once. About fifteen years ago all the clocks stopped at exactly one o'clock. Some of the clocks are battery powered and some are electric. How could this happen? Some say it was the ghosts. But why was this time chosen? Were they reliving an important moment in the mine's history? Perhaps a terrible accident occurred at one o'clock in the afternoon many years before and the shockwaves recur at intervals throughout time.

Perhaps the strangest phenomenon at the Gold King Mine happened at the former boarding house and bordello. This building sits precariously on a hill and is no longer accessible to visitors. The building was used as a bordello until the 1950s when Jerome was finally abandoned. Traces of wallpaper and empty shells of beds are seen throughout the building. A bullet hole is still visible on the second story of the house, a grim reminder of a more violent time in the town's history. Today everything is eerie and silent as the wind sweeps through the open windows. Years ago Don used to take the staff, about four or five people, to dinner in Cottonwood or Jerome. When they left the site they would lock the big gate up front to prevent trespassers. When they returned and unlocked the gate, they would see the old boarding house all lit up as if someone was having a big party. So they would all hurry up to the house and by the time they got there, the lights were out and the house empty and quiet. It is odd enough that the house was lit up without a single living soul around, it is odder still as there is no electricity in the old building. How did this happen? Is it another scene from the past, with the ghosts partying eternally? This occurred a number of times in the past, but no longer seems to happen. Perhaps the revelers have finally completed their sentences on this earth. Or are they just resting up for other evenings? The ladies of the night seem to have returned to wander around their former home. One visitor swore she saw a couple of the girls lifting up their skirts and washing themselves at the water trough.

While you are in Jerome, take the time to drive up the Perkinsville Road which will take you to the former town of Haynes, the Gold King Mine and Ghost Town. Be sure to see the authentic mine shaft, enter the mine itself, roam around the historic buildings, and view the bordello up on the hill. You will also have a great panorama of the Verde Valley. If you stay for awhile, a time storm may catch you and the past days of Haynes come alive. You might just see a miner, a lady of the night or other apparitions from the past because in this ghost town the former inhabitants return eternally.

7

Prescott
The Missing Priest
And a Haunted Hotel

Prescott, Arizona is situated on a beautiful mesa bordered by the Prescott National Forest and surrounded by mountains. High above Prescott towers Thumb Butte, jutting into the crystal blue skies like an ancient, ruined castle. The steep creviced walls often look like scorched rust in sunlight. It can be seen some distance away and has always been a landmark of this town. While Prescott was once the capital of Arizona, today it is known for its mild weather and is a popular retirement community. But retirees are not the only ones who flock to Prescott and find it hard to leave; ghosts also inhabit this old southwest town. When you visit, heed particularly the local theater, where you might spy a shadowy form moving across the stage, and the Hotel Vendome, where you might hear the rhythmic purring of a long-dead feline, who is still comforting Abby, the resident ghost of Room 16.

In 1863, when Arizona was named a territory of the United States, it was determined that the capital should be near Fort Whipple, where gold had recently been found. General James H. Carleton told the Governor's party to look for the Thumb Butte as a landmark for the site that would be used for the new territorial capital. Several names were suggested for this town, but it was decided to name it after William Hickling Prescott, a famous historian of the time.

Prescott was the capital of the Arizona Territory until 1867 when Tucson assumed the honor. It was moved back to Prescott in 1887, and then moved permanently to Phoenix in 1889. The mines largely influenced the early years of Prescott. After first finding gold in and around Prescott, silver veins were also found nearby. The gold and silver mines were very lucrative initially but eventually were drained. However, all was not lost as copper was found southwest and east of Prescott.

Although Prescott was only a capital city for a short period of time, the city was planned very carefully. A large square in the center of town was set aside for public buildings and a plaza. As with all Wild West towns, even grand ones like Prescott, there was a "Whiskey Row". Montezuma Street was where all the saloons were situated and at the turn of the twentieth century there were forty saloons here. This was the center of night life, gambling and drinking. Late at night, wandering the streets of Prescott, the dark shadows of the old buildings and the lonely, dry wind riding across the mesa, might cause you to see an eerie red glow in some windows and catch the scent of burning timbers. Then you are moving through time to the old Prescott. This phenomenon occurs in many of the former mining towns in Arizona. Perhaps the ancient, desert landscape of Arizona has mummified the brief lives of these towns.

Possibly the most famous event in the history of Prescott was the fire of July 14, 1900. Before this fire Prescott was booming, businesses were doing well, and the railroad had arrived. Some people believe that the fire started at the Scopel Hotel, others at the Miners' Home next door. In either case it seems that a candle was left burning, a strong gust leaped the flames into the curtains, and within minutes the building was on fire. To make matters worse, this was the height of the summer, and the reservoirs were nearly empty. When the fire hoses were connected to the hydrants no water came out. Unhampered, the fire quickly spread throughout downtown, and with no water available, the only way to stop the fire was to demolish the buildings in its path. In the course of five hours, three and half blocks of the business district were destroyed, including all of Whiskey Row. Not to be discouraged, businesses started setting up on the plaza immediately, with tents and shacks. Prescott simply rebuilt the downtown bigger and better than before the fire. Today 637 buildings in Prescott are on the National Register of Historic Places. However, there is at least one spirit that relives the night of the fire over and over again.

One of the buildings on the National Register of Historic Places is the former Church of the Sacred Heart of Jesus. It was constructed from 1891 until dedication on February 17, 1895. The church was built in the Sober Gothic Style with arched windows and beautiful stained glass windows, including circular ones high on the side walls. From these windows a murky light dimly illuminates the pressed tin walls and ceiling. The sanctuary of the church is semi-circular and is now the stage in the building's new life as a theatre. The steeple rose 115 feet, but sadly was struck by lightning and never replaced.

Prescott Fine Arts Association

The Sacred Heart Church served Prescott until 1969, when the congregation moved to a new, much larger church a few blocks away. In 1968 the Prescott Fine Arts Association (PFAA) was formed, but it did not have a home. When the Sacred Heart Church was vacated in 1969, the PFAA leased the building for the summer, and presented five productions during its three-month occupancy. In late 1969 the Church became the permanent home for the Association and is still used as a theatre and a gallery. At first the art exhibits were hung on the walls of the theatre, finally the lower level of the building was converted into a gallery and gift shop. To this day performances continue, although all is not tranquil; the former church and adjoining rectory seem to be haunted.

Reverend Father Edmond Clossen was a roaming Catholic Priest who did not have a regular parish. He spent a lot of time in Prescott visiting with Father Quetu of the Sacred Heart Church and staying in the second floor rooms of the rectory. When the fire broke out in downtown Prescott in 1900, Prescottonians came running to the rectory asking for help. Father Clossen woke up at the cries for help and attempted to wake up a fellow priest who was sleeping in a locked bedroom at the top of the stairs. He knocked and banged repeatedly on the door, shaking and rattling the door and yet this priest (whose identity has been lost over time) did not wake up. Finally Father Clossen abandoned his attempts to waken his fellow priest and went out to give solace to the masses.

When Father Clossen died two years later on June 18th,

1902 his body was brought to Sacred Heart Church and was buried beneath the altar. Strangely his death certificate has never been found. When the church was converted into the theatre, a permit was issued for Father Clossen's body to be moved to a local cemetery on September 17, 1969. However, when the Sacred Heart Parish excavated under the altar they did not find his remains.

As with many stories of hauntings there are variations of this tale, as if ghosts purposely disturb the memories of witnesses to hide their true identities. Some say the priest died while ministering to the tribes in the areas around Prescott. Did the priest die at the hands of local tribes angry at a man in black defaming their ancestors and now the priest drifts like desert sand throughout the safety of his church? Or did the native people find him dying in the heat of the desert and bring him back to die in the cool sanctuary of the church, respecting his beliefs? The truth seems lost in the receding past but what is true is the presence in the church and rectory.

Even though his remains are no longer on the premises, it seems that Father Clossen has not really left the Sacred Heart Church. To this day the frantic sounds of Father Clossen trying to awaken the priest sleeping through the fire are heard over and over again. The clambering at the door is heard from the dressing rooms down below. (The room the un-responsive priest slept too soundly in is now used for costume storage and a dressing room is directly beneath it.) Zach Hirsch, who has been involved with the theatre for over twenty-two years, heard the rattling once while he was in the men's dressing room downstairs. He decided to investigate the noise. There was no one upstairs and the door was shut to the costume room. No wind caused the door to rattle as the window was closed, and when he shook it, it did not rattle. He was confounded, there seemed to be no earthly source for the rattling noise of the door.

Down the hall from this haunted costume room, Bert Elizabeth Ijams, Director of The Prescott Performing Arts Association, has an office, which seems to share some of the hauntings. Her office used to have a very foul smell, especially at sunset; it was so bad it made her nauseous. One day, after months of this unpleasant phenomenon, she simply asked the presence to leave, and has not been bothered by it since. Apparently, this spirit needed only a command to be gone, a very accommodating soul, indeed. Once in her office, when she was alone in the building, she saw someone walking down the hall, just a shadowy form, but still a presence. When she searched the hall and the rooms there was no one. Because of these disturbing experiences Bert does not like to be alone in her office at night.

In the theatre itself, Bert says she has felt unsettled at times. One day she felt every hair on her body stand up while on the stage (this is where the altar used to be, and Father Clossen's supposed burial space). She found this a very uncomfortable experience. Bert still gets chills when she revisits this spot, including during my tour with her of the theatre.

Ghostly apparitions have appeared in the theatre. This is

not surprising, as theaters are well known to be favorite resting spots for spirits. The PFAA's theatre seems more prone than most to activity as it also is a former church. Perhaps it is Father Clossen's shadowy form that has been seen passing in front of the set. Was it Father Clossen who one night lifted three glasses from the bar on stage and dropped them to the floor? This occurred after a nightly performance of the play Blithe Spirit, when the director and three actors were on-stage checking the set for the following day's performance. Was he showing his disapproval of the play on his resting space? Perhaps he was just showing his amusement at the subject matter considering he is a spirit as well. Is Father Clossen responsible for problems with the intercom system between the light booth and the stage where telephone calls, radio broadcasts, and even babies crying are heard? Perhaps we will never know for certain, but it seems likely that this roving priest, whose final resting place remains a mystery, has been drawn back to the Sacred Heart Church.

The Prescott Fine Arts Association building is not the only location with ghosts in Prescott. Several of the hotels in town are reported to be haunted including the Hassayampa Inn, the Head Hotel, the Lynx Creek Farm Bed and Breakfast, and the Hotel Vendome, which is the most famous as Abby Byr and her cat Noble are haunting Room 16 forever, waiting for her husband to return.

The Hotel Vendome is just a short walk from Courthouse Plaza and Whiskey Row, yet it is a peaceful and quiet hotel. In 1917 Jack Jones, a rancher, moved to Prescott, bought a house for himself, and began construction on a thirty room hotel on the lot adjacent to his house. He named his hotel the Hotel Vendome, although it is uncertain where he came up with the name. Through the years the hotel changed hands many times. Today it is on the National Register of Historic Places and open as a charming bed and breakfast inn. It has a cozy lobby full of stuffed chairs and plants, with a small bar and big windows looking out onto the street.

Besides being a delightful historic hotel, with a wonderful location in the heart of Prescott, the Hotel Vendome is known for one other thing: the ghosts of Abby Byr and her cat Noble. Legend says that Abby Byr was a former owner of the hotel, although this has never been proven, since a complete list of owners is known and her name does not appear. Some say she may have been a manager, although her name does not appear on these records either. In fact, her name appears nowhere in any of the records that exist on the history of Prescott at Sharlot Hall Museum. It appears that the name Abby Byr was first used in 1983, perhaps the discovery of some guests with the use of a Ouiji Board. However, even if her name is not accurate, the stories of the haunting have remained consistent over the years. As no other name is known, we shall just use the names Abby and Noble for the ghosts of the Vendome.

It is believed that Abby lived and died at the hotel in the early 1920s. Legend says that she was very ill with tuberculosis and her husband left the hotel one night to either get a doctor or medicine. In either case, he never returned. In despair Abby locked herself and her beloved cat in her room, number 16; they both perished a short time later. It is said that the cat is buried in the back yard of the hotel, although no attempts to find it have been made. The final resting place of Abby is unknown.

Stories of the hauntings in the hotel go back to the 1930s; by the 1940s and 1950s visitors would come by the hotel hoping for a sighting of the famous ghosts. Tales abound of a black cat ghost scurrying up the steps and a female spirit gliding mysteriously throughout the hotel. Since the hotel's restoration in 1983 spirit activity, or at least reports of spirits, have increased. It often seems that restoring a property will increase or start ghostly activity. Souls trapped within a location, unable to move on, become distressed when changes occur to their former homes. Perhaps this is the case at the Hotel Vendome.

It appears that during the early 1980s Abby acquired her name, and Room 16 was the hot spot of sightings. Initially, hotel managers tended to leave Room 16 as the last one to be rented. Today Room 16 has to be booked months in advance; the room alone is a tourist destination. You can read the notes of hotel visitors in a large binder, which is kept behind the front desk. When Abby's Room is unoccupied you might just be given a peek and you can see the items that countless guests have left for Abby and Noble, including clothing, figurines, and cat toys. There is a feeling of memorial in the room, maybe from all of the gifts left in homage to the departed.

Room 16 is not alone in having other world visitors. Ghostly phenomena have been reported in other rooms, at the Hotel Vendome as well, including Room 26 where one visitor lying in bed saw a woman in a "gray outfit with puffy sleeves, a puffy hat, and a white apron over her shoulders, pull the cover over her." The spectral woman then started to walk away and then vanished instantly. A strong fragrance accompanied this apparition. And the visitor noted that she felt a heaviness overcome her and she could not move, only observe in shock the walking ghost.

Some people claim that a male spirit resides in the hotel. Perhaps this is Abby's husband, finally returning to her after all these years. It is sad to think that these two spirits have yet to connect in their forlorn wanderings in the hotel. A strong perfume has also been sensed throughout the hotel, described as gardenias or roses, suggesting a trail left by the presence of Abby as she seeks her husband. One night, a man walking up the stairs realized what he thought was his shadow was not in sync with his movements. Then a luscious perfume overwhelmed him followed by a frosty chill as if some presence had glided up the stairs.

Poltergeist-type activities are common at the Vendome. In the lobby of the hotel, the bell at the front desk rings when no one is there. The clock in the lobby never worked for years, but now every once in awhile it will chime at the correct time. Doors throughout the hotel will sound like they have been slammed closed when they are already locked. Footsteps are heard on the stairwell when no one is around. Throughout the hotel you may hear a cat scratching or purring even though there is no cat living here.

However, the heart of the haunting is in Room 16. Guests staying here have reported feeling a large cat jump on the bed, make three circles, and then lie down. The presence is described as warm and furry. Ceiling fans, lights, and the television will mysteriously turn on and off in the room, doorknobs will rattle, and the closet door where Noble is supposed to have died will close by itself. The sounds of a cat scratching at the closet door and meowing softly can also be heard. Also the hangers in the closets every so often move on their own. The bathroom in Room 16 has a lot of activity too. Most commonly the light is reported to turn on and off on its own and the door opens and closes on its own. Chills and a strong presence are also felt in this room.

Prescott, Arizona is a welcome relief from the heat of the Phoenix area in the summer. The fresh mountain air and dry conditions have long made this a sanctuary for people with ill health. Prescott is becoming a paradise for retirees, who enjoy the climate and the town's historic feel. While in Prescott take in a play at the Prescott Performing Arts Association Theater, and watch for an odd shadow at the back of the stage, it might be Father Clossen. Spend the night at the Hotel Vendome and try to comfort the unearthly presence of a lonely spirit and her cat, seeking solace and companionship long after their deaths.

Vulture Mine wooden head frame

8

Vulture Mine
Shadows from the Hanging Tree

It became the richest gold mine in nineteenth century Arizona, but Vulture Mine's history is full of grief, misery, and death. Murder and theft punctuated the sad saga of this small mining town. Riches were stolen by miners and gangs, the founder of the mine died penniless of a self-inflicted gunshot wound, and countless miners died in cave-ins and under falling timbers as they burrowed greedily after more and more gold. It is no wonder that so many spirits still cause trouble in this old west mining town outside of Wickenburg.

On entering the mine site, you encounter the front wall

of a large gray building fallen face down. Try standing in one of the broken windows and you might feel the rush of the wall as it fell flat onto the desert dust. As you wander the ghost town, right away you feel the presence of the departed everywhere. There are aged buildings throughout the mine founded by Henry Wickenburg. He was born in Austria in 1820 and moved to America, initially settling in California during the gold rush. He eventually made his way to Arizona, and under the advice of a rancher named King Woosley, searched the Harquahala Mountains for gold. Here in 1863 Wickenburg found his gold, twelve miles west of the Hassayampa River. Legend says that when Wickenburg struck gold he looked up and saw vultures circling around and thus the name of the strike, and later the town was formed.

Vulture Mine was yet another lonely outpost of mining in the great stretch of Arizona. There is a great silence in the surrounding desert, a silence of eons. Imagine working hours in the bowels of the mine and emerging in the dark night, your back feeling broken and there to greet you is the desert wind howling nothing. That is why whiskey was so comforting, though your arms ached so much you could barely lift the glass; and stealing gold made sense, as a way of escaping, though it most often led to a hangman's noose.

Unlike many men who found gold, Wickenburg preferred to outsource the difficult mining work. The Vulture Mine was a lode mine, meaning that the gold was still attached to the ore. Wickenburg sold the ore for fifteen dollars a ton, and let the buyers do the mining, transporting, and milling on their own. Shortly after his discovery a boomtown arose, called Vulture City. In 1866 Benjamin Phelps bought an eighty percent interest in the mine. However, it is believed that he never paid Wickenburg the price they agreed on, thus leading to Wickenburg's downfall. It is said Wickenburg only received twenty thousand dollars of the agreed eighty-five thousand dollars. Wickenburg then tried ranching, but was unsuccessful at that, and penniless, he shot himself to death in 1905.

Sadly the founder of the mine never enjoyed the vast riches the Vulture Mine had hidden. In the first six years of Phelps working the mine more than 2.5 million dollars in gold was supposed to have been extracted. However the actual amount of gold is thought to have been far greater than this. It is believed that as much as forty percent of the Vulture Mine's gold was "high-graded," that is pocketed by the miners themselves. It is believed that eighteen of these thieves were strung up on the hanging tree in Vulture City.

In 1878 James Seymour bought the Vulture Mine despite strong feelings from the locals that the veins had long since been mined out. Seymour was correct in his assessment that the Vulture Mine still had much to offer and it thrived for many years. The post office in Vulture closed in 1897, but only in 1942 did the mine itself close for good when President Roosevelt banned mining of non-strategic materials during World War II.

During the height of the mine's production, Vulture became the third largest city in the Arizona Territory, swelling to five thousand people. This meant a dramatically increased need for food. Interestingly the solution lay sixty miles to the south in a small agricultural community in the Salt River Valley, called Phoenix. The increased need for food and supplies in Vulture Mine, now grown to become Vulture City, helped to fuel the growth of Phoenix, which would of course become the largest city in Arizona.

Ultimately, Vulture Mine would produce over two hundred million dollars worth of gold, although times were never easy in Vulture City. The gold created fortunes but also spawned thieves and murder. On March 19, 1888 when three thousand dollars worth of gold bullion was being transported to Phoenix, the bandit Francisco Vega and his gang attacked the team delivering the gold. The two men carrying the gold, one of whom was mine superintendent Cyrus Gribble, were killed. Ultimately three members of the gang were found, as was the gold bullion, but the illusive Francisco Vega was never found and disappeared into infamy.

In 1923 tragedy would strike the Vulture Mine when several miners chipped ore out of the rock walls, which helped to support the mine, and brought one hundred feet of rock onto their heads. (It is said they were doing some "personal mining" at the time.) Ultimately seven miners and twelve burros (donkeys) died from this incident, creating a large depression known today as the Glory Hole. This was named because these miners were sent on to glory in this tragic accident.

Today Vulture Mine is open to tourists. It is remarkable

as a true example of a ghost town with a large collection of surviving buildings. Visitors can walk all around the town and into the buildings themselves. Be careful around the Glory Hole and the main mine shaft of the Vulture Mine, whose wooden head frame is still perched overtop. Looking down into the dark shaft, you may feel a cold breath rise from the depths as if the mine is panting and alive. Visitors can also visit the Assay Office, which was constructed from low-grade ore and is believed to contain six thousand dollars worth of gold and silver in its walls. Other buildings include the blacksmith shop, the ball mill, bunkhouses, the old mess hall, and two old schoolhouses. With all of these surviving buildings and the tragedies that occurred in town, it is no wonder that many believe the Vulture Mine is not completely abandoned. Ghosts still call this former boomtown home.

During my visit to the Vulture Mine in February 2007, I was struck by how large the town is and how well preserved the buildings are. Inside the Assay Office (the building where they would test the purity of metals being mined) there is a bed frame in the bedroom upstairs, sitting, waiting for an occupant. A table and chairs linger in the downstairs living room and an old pair of boots leans against the wall with a tattered shirt resting on a hook above. It is said that several people were killed while attempting to rob the assay office, and that this is one of the most active areas in the town. Visitors have seen apparitions of miners. Sudden unexplained temperature changes are experienced, and some, even on the hottest of days, feel a rush of cold air. One day a thirteen-year-old girl started to tour the Vulture Mine with her parents, and entered the Assay Office, as it is the first stop on the walking tour. She came immediately back to the Vulture's Roost (the building where you pay your admission). She said the Assay Office was full of ghosts and refused to tour the rest of the town, instead waiting in the Roost for her parents to finish their tour. It is said that animals are sometimes more sensitive to activity from the other side, and this appears to be the case in the Assay Office. On many occasions visitors with dogs find that their pets refuse to enter this building.

Assay Office

The Vulture's Roost itself has hauntings of its own. Usually the activity in this building involves objects being moved around after it is locked up for the night. One morning the manager found a stool moved to the middle of the entrance with art supplies piled up perilously on top. Shadowy figures have also been seen going across the room in front of the door.

This shadowy form has been seen by Kris Anderson, who has been managing the Vulture Mine for the past thirteen years. He has also seen lights in the buildings at night even though they have no electricity.

The Power Plant is also said to be haunted. Someone was killed there in the past by the flywheel. One day when Kris was in this building, he had his picture taken and in the developed photo was a figure of a man standing beside him, even though there was no one next to him at the time. Was this the poor soul who lost his life so tragically in this accident?

The Hanging Tree

95

The Mess Hall is another haunted building in Vulture City, with strong aromas of coffee being sensed by many visitors. The coffee cans on display are empty, and it has long since closed its doors to serving meals.

Near the end of the walk around town, you find the hanging tree. It is said that many men were hanged from this tree for high grading, rape, and murder. The tree is gnarled and misshapen, as if bent with its own history. And no wonder - while no records were ever kept to let us know the names of these men, legend says that at least eighteen people lost their lives on this tree. There is a feeling of despair under the bowed limbs of the tree; it seems cold like you just stepped into a meat locker. You may not want to linger at this tree. One can imagine shadowy forms around this tree, with their screams echoing into eternity.

A short drive away from the main town site sits the two schoolhouses of Vulture City. The swings, slide, and teeter-totters are a quiet reminder of the children who studied in these buildings. Peering into the buildings from outside, rows and rows of desks can be seen. These buildings also harbor ghosts, as many visitors say they see children in and around these buildings, and hear the sounds of children laughing and playing by the swings and slide. Images of children are supposed to appear in photographs taken of the old school houses. Sadly I was unable to capture any such image on film, and the only child I heard was my son. However, one can imagine the shadowy form of a ghostly child laughing going down the slide, and swinging on the swings, screaming "higher, higher". Vulture Mine was hit with waves of influenza and many children perished. You may also hear faint low rounds of coughing of the children from the cemetery. Let us believe that they are able to have fun eternally in the playground and their suffering is forgotten.

The Vulture Mine is a fabulous example of a true Arizona ghost town, with many buildings to visit and many ghosts to encounter. Most of the buildings have a treasure trove of artifacts everywhere, almost as if the town was abandoned suddenly, or everything was left for the ghosts. It is believed that a large amount of gold still remains in the mine, and if the current owners get their wish and sell Vulture Mine, mining might resume again one day. We can only hope that the town and its old buildings will remain open to visitors so we can have a glimpse into the past of Arizona, and see what remains of this former boomtown. Vulture Mine is an outstanding example of the Wild West, without the usual touristy gimmicks; here you truly feel you are back in the old days, and for a little while at least, can hear the vultures call and ghosts speak.

Hotel San Carlos

9

Phoenix
Haunted Dining

As the largest city in Arizona, Phoenix has much to offer. The greater Phoenix area has a population of nearly four million people, forty percent of whom live in the city of Phoenix itself. The rest of the area is made up of over twenty smaller cities whose boundaries all run together. Phoenix is the fifth largest city in America (and this is only taking the population of Phoenix proper into consideration). It is the headquarters of many companies, and plays host to major sporting events, concerts, and sports teams. It has world class resorts and golf courses, and is known for its wonderful dry and warm winters, and scorching summers. Lesser known is that Phoenix is also the home to several ghosts who seem to have a peculiar fondness for dining in the desert city.

Phoenix is different from many large American cities in that it has a relatively young history. The Hohokam Indians were the first residents of the Valley and lived here for seven hundred years before they mysteriously disappeared in 1400 A.D. The ruins of Phoenix's first people can be seen at Pueblo Grande, near downtown Phoenix. A visit on a hot summer day makes you appreciate what these first desert dwellers had to deal with in their struggle for survival in the Valley of the Sun. It would be almost five hundred years before it would be inhabited again.

In 1865 Fort McDowell was established near present day Phoenix. When Lt. John Y.T. Smith left the army he decided to stay in the area as a hay contractor. Fields of wild hay flourished on the floodplains of the Salt River. He set up camp, and the area became known as Smith's Station. The laborious task of clearing out the old canals that the Hohokam had made, began in 1867, and by 1868 wheat and barley crops had been planted. The canal system became known as the Town Ditch and was used for drinking water, irrigation, washing laundry, and bathing. By the end of 1868 the population was fifty people, and by 1870 it had reached just over 200 people. As the population grew the residents decided to plan an official town site, and while there were several suggestions, the town center ended up in a parcel between today's 7th Street and 7th Avenue. A name for the new town was needed and Phoenix was chosen as this town rose from the ashes of a previous civilization, just as the mythical bird rises from its own ashes.

Despite the growing number of residents, water was still an issue in this dry desert town, and in 1885 William Murphy began construction on the thirty five mile long Arizona Canal. The canal was completed in June 1887, and later a cross-cut canal connecting all of Phoenix's canals was constructed. With a reliable water supply, Phoenix's population continued to rise, and in 1889 Phoenix became capital of Arizona. The Arizona Canal helped with Phoenix's water problems, but bad floods in 1890 and 1891 nearly wiped out the small town. To ensure its future Phoenix looked to Washington for help and in 1902 the National Reclamation Act was passed, and the Salt River Valley was the first area chosen to help under the plan. The result of this act was the Roosevelt Dam, completed in 1911, and four more dams were built over the years. Now the future of Phoenix was assured. Federal funds in 1926 provided paved highways around Arizona bringing this Wild West State into the 20th century. Today thousands of people relocate to Phoenix every year inspired by the desert landscape, sunny skies, and advancement opportunities. With such a modern city it is hard to imagine that there is much from its brief past that remains lingering, but several spirits have found it impossible to leave the Valley of the Sun. Come to Phoenix and you will see why it is so hard for some to leave.

In the heart of old Phoenix sits Heritage Square. Here you will find a small collection of old houses that give you a glimpse of what life was like in this small town at the turn of the century. In one of these houses you might also be able to see a ghost.

The Teeter House today is a pleasant tea house where you can enjoy a light meal or full tea. At night you can enjoy a jazz concert and have a drink under the stars on the patio, or inside in one of the cozy rooms. But all is not quiet at this tea house. The Teeter house was built in 1899 by Leon Bouvier, a cattleman and flour miller who operated the house as a boarding house. In 1911 he sold the property to Eliza Teeter who continued to operate the home as a boarding house until 1919 when she moved into the three bedroom home herself and stayed there until she died in 1965.

The house is a cozy bungalow with gleaming woodwork, floral wallpaper, fireplaces, and lace curtains. Besides being a full service restaurant and tea house, the Teeter House also operates as a gift shop, with unique gifts including teapots. One item that might not be on the menu is the spirit of Eliza Teeter herself who, after living in her home for so many years, seems unwilling to leave.

Numerous odd occurrences take place at the Teeter House including people hearing their names in soft whispers and objects moving by themselves. One of the most dramatic events was when a roll of paper towels in the restroom began to unroll by itself spilling onto the floor. The kitchen also seems haunted as pots and pans have flown off the shelves. Once a cook saw a woman walk casually through the restaurant before completely disappearing as if stepping into nowhere. Another time a cook heard her name called, when no one else was in the building. A shelf in the dining room has been thrown across the room, and once the owner's keys were placed under the kitchen sink. Could Eliza Teeter just be trying to get some attention? Does she approve of all the activity in her former home? Perhaps she just wants to join the party. While we may not know Eliza Teeter's motive in haunting her former home, it seems this spirit of old Phoenix is here to stay.

Moving east from downtown Phoenix we travel to downtown Tempe. Today Tempe is well known as the home of Arizona State University, and has a vibrant historic downtown area, full of restaurants and shops. It is also home to two haunted restaurants.

Casey Moore's Oyster House is on a leafy green residential street just a few steps away from historic downtown Tempe. The restaurant is in an old house which was built in 1910 by William Moeur. The house was a boarding house in the 1930s and for a brief spell a brothel as well, then it was a fraternity house, and in the 1980s it was turned into a restaurant. The restaurant has seen a lot of unexplained activity over the years. The misty forms of the original owners, William and Mary Moeur, have been observed many times dancing in an upstairs window, including by neighbors who live across the street. Of course the ghostly dances take place when the restaurant is closed, and no one is present in the building. The police have even been called in the past to investigate the intruders, but of course they find no one there.

Casey Moore's Oyster House

Other spirits that reside in the building can perhaps be linked to Casey Moore's brief life as a brothel. A couple of friendly spirits like to flirt and play with those at the restaurant. Ghostly laughter echoes around the restaurant at night. A favorite activity of these spirits is to rearrange the tables and chairs. On one occasion the chairs were all lined up with the plates stacked on top. Other times food and utensils are thrown on the floor while faint giggling can be heard. These seem to be playful spirits.

One of the most dramatic events was when a painting in the dining room flew off the wall in front of a packed room of patrons. No explanation could be found. Employees have also heard their names being called when they are alone in the building. And the alarm system has turned on for no reason, no earthly reason at any rate. It seems that no one is ever really alone at Casey Moore's Oyster House, and it seems likely to stay that way. For a wonderful meal and some lively atmosphere give Casey Moore's a try. Better yet, stroll by the restaurant in the middle of the night, and you too might witness the couple dancing in the upstairs window, enjoying their waltz into eternity.

Just up the street from Casey Moore's is Monti's La Casa Vieja. The history of Monti's is linked with the history of Tempe itself. The original adobe house was constructed in 1871 by Charles Trumbull Hayden. Hayden established a ferry to cross the Salt River, and the community became known as Hayden's Ferry; subsequently the area was renamed Tempe.

Hayden eventually became a congressman. His former home is the oldest continuously occupied structure in the Phoenix metropolitan area.

Hayden's house has served as a hotel, a blacksmith shop, a post office, and a general store. By the 1890s, it became known as *La Casa Vieja* - the old house. It was also in the 1890s that the first restaurant was operated in the building. The house was purchased in 1954 by Leonard F. Monti Sr., who opened his restaurant in 1956. The restaurant, now on the National Register of Historic Places, is filled with memorabilia. The restaurant is also filled with phantom presences from the other side.

Over the years numerous reports have been made of otherworldly patrons visiting the restaurant. One of the most common sights has been of a cowboy in the Mural Room. He stands there and then disappears slowly before your eyes. In the Fountain Room the faint sound of children's laughter can be heard. With such a long history it isn't surprising that ghosts are on the menu at Monti's. This old house is haunted indeed.

The last haunted restaurant we will visit is in Mesa, Arizona, and also has a long history. The Landmark Restaurant was built as a Mormon Church in 1908. At the time the building was smaller than what is seen today. In 1930 the church expanded, to look much as the restaurant does today. The congregation moved in the 1950s to a larger space and the building was taken over by an insurance company. In 1963 the building was used as the Mesa Community College. In 1972 the first restaurant opened on site, Rouch's Schoolhouse Restaurant. In 1981 the Landmark Restaurant opened. The building is filled with historic photographs and antiques chronicling the history of the building and Mesa.

Also helping to keep the history alive at the Landmark restaurant is the resident ghost. The spirit is most often experienced in the ladies room where the faucets turn on and off by themselves. Women also hear their name whispered from an unearthly voice. In the deserted downstairs hall, women's voices are heard. Just who is responsible for these ghostly voices is unknown, but if you visit the Landmark Restaurant you too might hear a faint whisper from beyond.

The most famous haunted building in Phoenix is the Hotel San Carlos. After visiting and dining at the haunted restaurants in the city, you can rest your weary head and full stomach at the only historic boutique hotel in the city. The downtown area where the Hotel San Carlos was built has a long history. The area was first used by the local Native Americans as a place to worship the God of Learning. This has led some to speculate that this is why this location was chosen for Phoenix's first school house. This small, one room adobe building was constructed in 1874. In 1879 the building was replaced with one made of brick, and in 1893 it was expanded to have sixteen rooms. In 1916 the school was condemned, and declared unsafe. The site was proposed for a large hotel, nine stories high and three hundred rooms. This large hotel never materialized, but in 1927 the Hotel San Carlos was opened. The building was seven stories high making it the highest building in Phoenix. It was also luxurious for the time with amenities such as an elevator, air-conditioning, and hot and cold water to all guest rooms. The basement of the hotel had (and still does) the well that originally served the school on the property, and delivered fresh water to the hotel. The hotel was built in the Italian Renaissance Style, with marble floors in the lobby, crystal chandeliers, and copper doors on the elevators. Preservation efforts through the years have placed the hotel on the list of Historic Hotels of America.

Tragedy befell the Hotel San Carlos early in its history when on May 7, 1928 twenty-two year old Leone Jensen jumped to her death off the roof of the hotel. Jensen had been staying in room 720. She wore a rose colored dress, as if she had been ready for a night of dancing. Her suicide note said that she killed herself after her love for a bellboy at a nearby hotel was unrequited. Her spirit is still felt in room 720 and throughout the hotel. Guests report strange cold breezes and the cloudy form of a woman throughout the hotel. Today the housekeeping staff will not go to the seventh floor alone. On the seventh floor clock radios turn off and on by themselves and the paintings on the walls keep making themselves crooked, no matter how many times they are straightened out.

While Leone Jensen is the most famous ghost of the Hotel San Carlos she is not the only one. There have been numerous reports throughout the years that the spirits of several young children roam the halls of the hotel. Childish laughter can be heard echoing through the halls and small footsteps are heard running around. Yet there is never any earthly source for these strange sounds. The spirits of the children can be traced to the basement of the hotel and the well that still exists there. It is believed that sometime during the late 1890s three or four boys drowned in the well. Their spirits are felt throughout the hotel. Their presence is especially noted in the basement by staff of the hotel.

A visit to the Hotel San Carlos will give you a feel of what life was like in old Phoenix. The hotel was frequented by many Hollywood stars, including Mae West, Clark Gable, and Cary Grant. These celebrities' names can now be seen on the San Carlos star walk, which has a star for each famous movie star who stayed at the hotel. Try to spend the night in haunted room 720 and you might experience the spirit of Leone Jensen as she paces and ponders her final act, and pause as you hear ghostly children laughing as they run around the halls. While their lives may have been taken from them too soon, they are living their childhoods for eternity, romping and playing in the hotel.

A visit to Phoenix is a must for its mountain views, blue skies, and resorts. Unknown to many people is that a visit to Phoenix is also a must for those looking for ghosts. Spirits seem to congregate in historic buildings turned into restaurants and one very haunted hotel built over a spiritual well. Perhaps you will see a misty form as you walk the halls of the San Carlos, view a ghostly couple dancing at Casey Moore's or hear your voice called out at the Landmark Restaurant. Whichever haunted restaurant you choose to visit, you will certainly enjoy the food and might be fortunate enough to get some spirits not normally found on the menu.

IO

Goldfield Ghost Town and the Superstition Mountains
Legends of Lost Gold

At the base of the Superstition Mountains, forty-five miles east of Phoenix along the Apache Trail, sits the town of Goldfield, Arizona. While at first glance, it might appear that this is just another mining town turned into a tourist attraction, the lore and legends that surround Goldfield and the Superstition Mountains set this town apart. It is impossible to visit without hearing the stories of the Lost Dutchman Mine. It is also impossible to overlook the fact that there are ghosts here. The feeling of the supernatural is strong under the shadow of the towering Superstition Mountains even with the crowds in the town.

To understand the history of Goldfield, it is first necessary to understand the legend of the Lost Dutchman Mine, and the mysteries of the Superstition Mountains. The Superstition Wilderness Area encompasses 242 square miles of Arizona's rugged desert mountain terrain. Some peaks tower 6,000 feet above sea level and deep, twisted canyons dissect this vast region of the Sonoran Desert. Here you find the giant saguaro cactus and prickly pear along with ponderosa pine. A diversity of animals struggle to survive, including mule deer, javelinas, mountain lions, coyotes, and a variety of birds, reptiles and amphibians. It is a wilderness of surrealistic rock formations, high spires, exotic cacti, and dangerous canyons and is one of metro Phoenix's most picturesque hiking areas.

The Apaches believe the Superstition Mountains are the home of the Thunder God and for them it is a sacred place. In their worldview, if the Thunder God is disrespected, terrible things will happen. Indeed over the years countless people have gone missing and lost their lives in this mysterious mountain range. About once a year the Superstition Mountains rumble and yell, rattling windows, and scaring those in its vicinity of the wrath of the Thunder God. Of course these rumblings are actually earth tremors, but this was not known during the height of feverish activity and exploration of the mountains. Knowing the dangers that exist, why would individuals continue to delve deep into the depths of these cliffs and canyons? They were all looking for the elusive Lost Dutchman Mine.

The story of gold in the Superstition Mountains goes

back over four hundred years to the Spanish explorer Francisco Vázquez de Coronado. He and his conquistadors were looking for gold, and seeking *las Siete Ciudades Doradas de Cíbola.* When they arrived in the area, they demanded that the local Apaches help them find gold. The Apaches refused, telling the Spanish if they dared to trespass on the holy ground, the Thunder God would take revenge, inflicting awful suffering and horrible deaths for them all. Discounting these stories of the Thunder God, Coronado and his army entered the mountain range anyway, but the Superstition Mountains have a way of getting to people. Soon strange accidents started to happen. The conquistadors and their horses fell into deep ravines, suffering deadly injuries. Men began to vanish mysteriously, as if captured by unseen forces, and soon the men were warned not to stray away from the army. Still, more and more of the Spanish force disappeared and many were later found dead. Some say the victims were found headless, adding to the terror of the mountains. Perhaps a few of these lost conquistadors still roam the gulches and ravines, their bones rattling against their rusted breast-plates. Do their eyes still glitter with the gold lust? Hikers speak of disturbing sounds and seeing shadows where there should be none. Perhaps the departed Spanish are only trying to find their way back to their fellow soldiers.

The thunderstorms that battered the mountains like cannon barrages were unlike anything the explorers had ever seen before, and they felt a strong fear, perhaps there was a Thunder God. Finally, the conquistadors fled, refusing to return to the mountain. Because of the eeriness of the place, Coronado gave it the name *Monte Superstition* and this is how the mountain range got its name.

Around 1700, the area was purportedly explored by the Jesuit priest Eusebio Francisco Kino. His main objective was to establish missions and Christianize the Native Americans. Some say he searched the region, finding gold. This added to the lore of treasure in the Superstition Mountains. His expeditions enraged the Apache, who began to keep trespassers off their sacred place.

In 1748, the Spanish King Ferdinand VI gave 3,750 square miles of Arizona to a Mexican cattle-baron, Don Miguel Peralta of Sonora, as a "church grant." This included the Superstitions. Supposedly the area contained several silver mines as well as a gold mine. For the next one hundred years, the Peralta family made only rare excursions from their home in Mexico to their property in Arizona. In 1845 Don Miguel Peralta, the then patron and descendent of the first Don Miguel, came to search vigorously for the legendary gold that eluded Coronado. Allegedly, he found a rich vein of gold and memorized the spot with the unique distinguishing landmark being a towering, hat-shaped peak he called *La Sombrera*. Of course, he therefore called the mine the Sombrero Mine. Peralta returned to Mexico to gather men and resources and eventually began shipping back large amounts of pure gold to Mexico. But by 1848 the Apache were angry at the presence of intruders on their sacred land, violating the domain of the Thunder God. Aware that an attack was coming Pedro Peralta (Don Miguel's son) concealed the mine, and then set out with bags full of gold. The Apaches got word of his route, and hid close by along the canyon and hills. No one survived the attack save a few pack animals with their heavy gold burden. The burros fled into ravines and washes with gold packed heavily in their saddlebags. The animals wandered and eventually died in the harsh desert mountain conditions. A few years later United States Army troops found several of the bloody bodies of the Peralta party and gave them a proper burial.

Later in 1848, Sean O'Connor and Aloysius Hurley, two army veterans, went looking for the legendary Peralta Gold Mine; while they did not find the mine, they did find several burro skeletons with disintegrated saddlebags, containing large amounts of gold. They sold what they found to the San Francisco Mint and received $37,000 (gold was worth $13.00 an ounce at that time). Certainly this gave credence to the existence of the Peralta Mine, but did not help with its location.

The next major event to occur in the Superstition Mountains, as far is gold is concerned, was the discovery of a mine by Jacob Waltz. For some reason Jacob Waltz has become known as the "Dutchman" when in fact he was a Deutchman from Germany. He was born in Werttemberg, Germany in July of 1810 and came to America in 1837. He spent some time in California before being lured to Arizona by tales of gold. Waltz began prospecting in the Bradshaw Mountains and in 1864 he and five other prospectors found gold in the Superstition

Mountains. But since they too had defiled the sacred land of the Thunder God, the Apaches attacked them, and all but two of the men were killed. One man who survived was Frank Brinkley, and the other was Jacob Waltz himself. Brinkley abandoned all thoughts of gold in the Superstition Mountains, but apparently Jacob Waltz did not.

In 1867 Waltz was one of the first settlers in Phoenix and acquired 160 acres of land near the river. He spent twenty-four years of his life living in his adobe house, raising chickens, but there were always rumors about where he had acquired the money to enable him to purchase the farm. Legend says that Waltz would appear in bars around Phoenix after periods of absence and pay for drinks with gold nuggets. When asked about his mine, Waltz would give contradictory directions and always eluded those who tried to follow him. But word about his mine began to spread. When he was drunk Waltz would boast that he knew of a mine that was rich enough to pave the streets of Phoenix in gold, yet no one could ever find his mine.

The luck of the "Dutchman" eventually ended when a disastrous flood occurred in 1891 destroying much of Phoenix, including the Waltz house. To save himself from drowning he climbed a tree and clung onto it all night, no easy task for an 81 year-old man.

The following day Rhinehart Petrasch, who worked for Mrs. Julia Thomas in her ice cream shop, rescued Waltz. Julia took Waltz in and let him live behind her business. The three individuals brought together by unusual circumstances became fast friends. As the year went on, Waltz became quite ill, and wanted to do something nice for his friends, so he told them about his gold mine. He said there was plenty of gold for everyone in his mine, which he confided was near the Superstition Mountains. He planned to take his friends to his mine, but was too sick to make the journey. As his condition became worse, he described the exact location of his mine to Julia and Rhinehart. He died on October 25, 1891.

So convinced was Julia about the location of the mine and the riches it had to offer she sold her ice cream shop and set out to find the mine with Rhinehart. However, what had seemed so clear in Waltz's description could not be followed in its execution. They could not find the mine. Rhinehart's brother Herman came to help in their search and they looked for two years, but could not find the gold. For over sixty years Herman searched the Superstition Mountains for the elusive mine, but could not find it. The searches concentrated on Weaver's Needle, but no mine was every found.

So where is the Lost Dutchman Mine? Weaver's Needle has always been thought of as a clue to the location of the mine, simply because Waltz's mine was near a peak. However, since so many people have searched this area over the years, this must be the wrong peak. Also, this land of towering peaks and deep canyons was formed by volcanic eruptions about twenty nine million years ago during the Tertiary Period of geologic time. It is composed of eroded lava, welded volcanic ash, and dacite tuff, which are essentially barren of gold and other metallic minerals.

This fact only seems to add more mystery to the legendary gold mine.

The description of where the mine is supposed to be is as follows: a short distance back from the western end of the main Superstition Mountains, high above a gulch and well concealed by brush, and the vein is eighteen inches wide with pure gold. So where is all the gold?

Superstition Mountains as seen from Goldfield

There is one area near the Superstition Mountains that has gold, and that is the area around Goldfield. Of interest is that historically Goldfield was considered as being in the Superstition Mountains. In 1891 four prospectors, J.R. Morse, C.R. Hakes, and Orrin and Orlando Merrill were searching for gold in the Superstition Mountains. They found the remains of an old mine, which they believed to be of Spanish origin; they located six claims on the site and recorded them in 1892. Later in 1892 five more claims were filed, and a Mr. Hall took control of the Black Queen Mine. In 1893 a sudden flash flood down the Superstition Mountains carried ten feet of water washing out sand, and taking out trees along its path. Hall went down the wash to get some lumber that had been taken away with the flood waters, and found some freshly exposed quartz; when it was crushed they found gold. This discovery was on the site of the Mammoth claim. This strike started a gold rush in the area. The Mammoth Mine was truly a bonanza mine, with very rich gold ore.

With such a discovery a town was soon formed, and took the name Goldfield. Over a short period of time buildings were erected, and a post office was established on October 7, 1893. The town had three saloons, a boarding house, and a schoolhouse. For four years the good times lasted, and the population around Goldfield swelled to four thousand people. But the mines closed in November 1897, although the reason for the closure is unknown. Boom and bust is the ever-present story of mining towns.

In 1910 the area had new life when George Young formed the Young Mine Company and drained the old mine of water. Through the years the Mammoth mine continued to produce and from 1921 to 1926 a post office returned, and Goldfield was known as Youngsburg. But when Young died the mine was left to rising water, and miners went over to work the Black Queen Mine. Here they found ore rich in gold, so rich that the miners practiced high grading (taking away some of the gold themselves every day). When the superintendent caught wind of what was happening he sent for the sheriff, the miners fled, and the mine closed down. There has been sporadic activity since this time, but in the early years of World War II, the Shumway Company bought the Goldfield claims and tore down all the buildings, sold all the machinery for scrap iron, and salvaged anything of value in the old ghost town.

But the quest for gold was not over yet for Goldfield; in 1948 Goldfield Mines Incorporated started mining again, diverting flood waters away with a large dam. Early on they found something unusual, a large slab of rock over an ancient mineshaft. Speculation arose that this was the Lost Dutchman Mine, or Peralta's Mine, or perhaps that they were the same thing. This pit once reopened revealed valuable ore, but by 1953 the pit reached sixty-five feet deep, too deep and steep to operate safely and the mining stopped. Now the pit is flooded, known only as Goldfield Pond.

One of the mines established in 1894 was the Bull Dog Mine, a site of huge riches, and it was beside a peak, Bull Dog Peak. So perhaps this peak was the one described by Waltz, and not Weaver's Needle. The peak has long ago been blown off, but it would explain the description of the Lost Dutchman Mine.

Whichever mine in the Goldfield region is the Lost Dutchman Mine, it seems likely that it is no longer lost, but has been mined, and that it is not in the midst of the Superstition Mountains.

Beyond the legends of the Lost Dutchman Mine are the ghost stories in Goldfield Ghost Town. While it seems most ghost towns have a ghost or two wandering around, this town seems to have more than its fair share. Perhaps this is because it lies in the shadows of the Superstition Mountains, and all the mystery and legends surrounding it descend to Goldfield. Whatever the cause is, it is certain this is one of the most haunted ghost towns in Arizona.

The ghosts of Goldfield haunt almost every building on the property and make themselves known in a variety of ways. The museum building is a particularly haunted spot, and I spent some time talking with Stephanie who manages the museum about the strange occurrences in the building. Stephanie started to work in the museum (which chronicles the search for the Lost Dutchman Mine) in October 2005. That Christmas at Goldfield she had her first strange experience. There is music played around the town over speakers, and at Christmas time, they play Christmas music. On several occasions when Stephanie would walk out onto the porch of her building she would not hear Christmas music, but instead it would be Johnny Cash songs, especially Ring of Fire. She asked the caretakers why they were playing Johnny Cash songs and they insisted they were not playing anything other than Christmas music. Stephanie explains, "a few years before this, I had lost my Dad, and that was one of his favorite songs. And I thought about how much he would have loved this place. Which is really unusual, and it's not like I was just thinking of him that day, it [the music] would just be there." Was her Dad trying to communicate with her and let her know that he was enjoying visiting the town from beyond?

Other strange experiences occur inside the museum including phantom footsteps from the closed-off second story of the building. Stephanie describes this event, "the first time I heard someone walking across the floor it was quite distinct, like someone wearing boots, and I thought that maybe I lost a customer. I went upstairs three times to see if I had lost someone up there, and no one was there. And the strange thing about it, you can see daylight through these slats, anytime that anyone walks up there, you get a little bit of dust that falls down, and sometimes small rocks too. And when he [the ghost] walks past back and forth the same thing happens. And there isn't anyone up there, there isn't anything up there."

These phantom visits on the second floor happen about once a month, but what old prospector is doing this eternal pacing is unknown. Before Stephanie started to work at the museum, the lights on the second story would turn themselves on. Once three nights in a row the lights on the second floor were on, yet the museum manager had not gone up there. Perhaps the phantom walker was interested in playing with the light, and has now grown bored of this. Even if the lights upstairs don't turn on by themselves anymore, there are still strange electrical disturbances in the museum. On a regular basis there is a problem with the cash register. Every once in a while the credit card machine will beep and start to feed itself paper; this is when it is not being used. This phenomenon has frightened several employees at the museum.

Stephanie traces this register activity to the death of a dear friend from the town, Karen, who had worked there for many years before passing away suddenly. This activity with the cash register began just a few weeks after her death. As Stephanie explains, "it was the only thing I could associate it with, because it had never done anything like that to me before. And when we lost her, it took everyone by surprise. And we weren't the closest of friends, but she knew that I never got out of my building, and she was the one person who cared enough to come in and give me a break." Perhaps Karen has never really left, and in her own way is still trying to give Stephanie a break.

The Mammoth Bar in town is a nice place to unwind,

enjoy a meal, some music and a drink. It is also a good place to witness a ghost. Joyce who lives and works at Goldfield was at the bar at Mammoth's one night when something made her turn around. The dining room lights were off, but when she turned she saw a shape go past the dance floor. She explains, "I never believed in ghosts or spirits…. but I could draw the shape of this thing. It was sort of like a Dick Tracy profile…it just floated, it was solid black. I don't know whether it was a legitimate manifestation or not." Joyce was not drinking at the time, so other spirits were not responsible for her seeing this spirit in the bar.

Joyce lives at Goldfield above the Blue Nugget building, and has over the years experienced many unexplained events in her home. The first odd occurrence was with the coffee maker. Every night Joyce gets the coffee maker ready for the next morning, but there is not a timer. For three or four nights in a row the coffee maker would turn on by itself at exactly 2:00 in the morning. On another occasion Joyce was taking a shower and she felt something grab her ankle. Even though the shower curtains didn't move, Joyce thought it must be her husband playing a trick on her, so she quickly pulled the shower curtain back, but her husband was asleep in bed. The floors creak and footsteps are heard throughout the house. Another strange event happened when Joyce was lying in bed. She explains, "I was sleeping on my left side, so I was facing the window. I felt the mattress sink down, you know like someone had come to lie down. I thought it was my husband. I turned around, there was no one there, and he was in the bathroom." The security door to their house also has a mind of its own. Every night they securely locked this door, and several times the next morning they would wake up and find the door wide open.

The haunted Blue Nugget

One of the oddest occurrences in the house involves a plant on the hutch. The good-sized potted plant was always on the left side of the hutch. In the morning the plant would be on the right side of the hutch, half off, half on in the perfect place of balance. Joyce says, "If you had blown on it, it would have crashed, that happened several times." In the store below their house, odd events have happened as well. Jewelry will move on its own over night from one end of the store to the other.

The experiences in her home were so frequent and disturbing that Joyce felt she needed to take action against the events in her home. She describes what she did to halt the events, "There was a guy up here who was a Shaman. This is a smudging stick. It stinks. What you do is light it, it is white sage and it is sacred. And you go around, especially in the corners and you pray them out and ask them to leave. So he did it, and I did it. And that seemed to have stopped the activity. That is what it is designed for." Joyce also buried a Bible under her house to further help ward off unwelcome spirits.

While the majority of the ghostly activity has stopped in Joyce's home, there are still odd events on occasion. Objects go missing only to turn up in a very obvious location just a short time later. During the week of my visit Joyce lost the antenna from her cell phone. She went out and bought another one, and came home to find her antenna lying neatly on the table in plain view. It had not been there when she left.

Strange odors also occur in her home, including cigar and cigarette smoke. Joyce says, "At night or during the day, especially when I am alone, I smell cigar smoke, or cigarette smoke. Now I had a grandfather that smoked cigars. The cigarette smoke, my son, he died about three years ago in a house fire, and he smoked. Whether or not that is related I don't know." Joyce has also smelled sulfur in her home.

While all of these manifestations and activity are disturbing at times, Joyce feels that they have an explanation. "Don't forget you are opposite the Superstition Mountain, and there is a lot of legends and lore about the mountain... I have heard of people who have encountered the Thunder God when they pack into the mountain. So to me, it is normal, because we live in the shadow of this mountain that any spirit manifestations or any spirit activity would fall to us."

The train station at Goldfield is also a hotbed of spirit activity. Sharon who manages the train station has had many odd experiences in the building. She has a loose-leaf binder for guest comments that sits nicely on a large wooden stand. This stand is now inside the middle of the building, but it used to be just inside the door. One day she came in and the binder was "flopping in the breeze" it was half way off the stand. She would have noticed the misplaced binder the night before if it was falling off the stand, but it wasn't. That same morning the lanterns on top of the piano had been rearranged from where they were the night before.

On one of Sharon's days off the station's engineer Alan called her at home and asked, "If before I left last night, I had moved the hat racks around. And I said no. The hat racks had

127

been moved to the point where you could not move between this display [of toy trains] and the hat racks. And one of the trains was in the middle of the floor. And we know that didn't happen before we left the night before because we would have tripped over it."

Goldfield Train Station

On another occasion it appears that a former employee was paying a visit from beyond. The father of the owner of the town of Goldfield, a man named Leroy, spent a lot of time at the train station. It appears that since his death he has not left the ghost town. Sharon came into work one day after the owner's Dad had passed away. By her cash register the calculator was moved, as was the receipt roll, the pile of scratch paper was in a fan, and there were lot of pens lying around. Sharon explains, "Now I have just five or six pens that I use, not an assortment. The owners Dad had this thing that if he was out and about and he needed to borrow a pen, like in a bank or wherever, he would just stick it in his pocket and take it home. And when I came in and saw this, I was thinking Leroy. The pens to me were a dead giveaway that he had been here to visit. For a while he used to work out here in the train station. But he would come and visit when he quit working here. He used to bring me pens because he had such a large collection of them. So that was a dead giveaway. And that happened probably within six months that he passed away." Also the day after Leroy died, Alan, the train engineer, reports that a cold gust of air shot down the mine.

Also in the train station the light goes out frequently in the machine that flattens pennies. However, when Sharon goes to replace the light bulb it hasn't burnt out, it just needs to be tightened. Alan experienced something strange with the ceiling lights one day. He explains, "I came in one day and one of the lights from the ceiling was broken. One piece was over here and one piece was over there. Just the insert fell out; the bulb was still up there. And they snap in, and none of them fall out. We super glued it back together again." On another occasion the alarm started to beep in the middle of the afternoon. It beeped three times, but the alarm was not activated, so there was no need for it to beep.

One of the entertaining things about Goldfield is that on weekends during the cooler months they reenact gunfights with actors. One time when a group of the gunfighters had their picture taken in front of the gallows a strange image appeared in the film. One of the gunfighters, Howie, explains, "When the picture was developed, the negative had an extra person to the left hand side. It didn't look like anything in the film. There has to be spirits around here. In the picture we can't tell if it's a woman or a man, but it is the outline of a figure behind the group."

Down Route 88, the Apache Trail, only a minute or so away from Goldfield is the Lost Dutchman State Park, where you can find trails into the Superstition Mountains, if you dare. Who knows, perhaps somewhere around the mountains the legendary gold may yet be found. But ghosts may be anywhere in the mountains; the low rattles you hear may not be rattlesnakes but the hoarse breathing of the many who have perished from the hunt for gold. The wind in the desert sounds like broken pottery shards, or shaken arrowheads, or a handful of bullets; but maybe it is only the wind sliding through the ocotillo and the creosote bushes. The Apache Trail itself is rich with big saguaros and fluffy cholla, yawning canyons and mountain vistas; be careful to watch the road too. The huge rock cliffs are burnt red and look like weathered ancient battlements. It's easy to imagine warriors eyeing you from their fortress in the sky.

But what is haunting Goldfield ghost town? Is it the souls of all those who sought in vain to find the Lost Dutchman Mine, and lost their lives during the search? Is it the spirits of lost family members whose love of the town and their family brings them back forever? Is it the spirits of the miners and others who lived, worked, and died in this town? The possibilities are endless. One early winter morning in Goldfield clouds clung close to the Superstition Mountains like wings or a cloak. Clouds are not common in the Valley of the Sun but they are around the Superstitions. There were only a few people in town. And then a harsh sound came from the clouds, perhaps rolling thunder, but it seemed like the grating of huge iron hinges. It sent a shiver through me. Were the ghosts coming out? The dusty street was small and lonely as dark shapes seemed to swarm everywhere. Then the feeling was gone. It was yet another strange event where strange things happen often. And what is the origin of all the specters, all of the odd happenings here? Perhaps we will never know for certain. But one thing is clear; this ghost town is very haunted. Visit Goldfield ghost town and enjoy the reconstructed buildings, the mine tour, pan for gold, or enjoy the shops and the saloon. But look carefully around, that might not be a gunfighter in costume after all, the ladies plying their trade in the bordello might not be modern re-enactors, and that figure you see creeping across the back of the saloon might not be from this time. For in the shadow of the Superstition Mountains it seems anything can happen in this ghost town.

131

Yuma Prison Dark Cell

II

Yuma Territorial Prison
Fear in a Dark Cell

Yuma, Arizona can trace its roots back over a thousand years to the time when the Quechan, Cocpah, Mojave and other Native American tribes farmed the rich land surrounding the Gila and Colorado rivers. During the winter months the land was fertile and rich, in the summer, it became unbearable, and these tribes would move to the cooler coastal mountains east of San Diego. This hot inhospitable climate made Yuma a perfect location for a prison. One would think former prisoners would not want to return after death; yet this prison still holds numerous lost spirits. Trapped in their cells many ghosts seem doomed to serve their sentences into eternity. And in the heat of this old Southwest Arizona penitentiary, you might feel the cold dying breaths of these prisoners or be touched by the wet, trembling fingers of a little girl still trying to save her doll from drowning.

Yuma is on the southwestern boundary of the state, close to Mexico and California. In 1780, Father Francisco Tomás Garcés established two missions in the Yuma area, but when gifts and respect promised to the Quechan tribes (also called the Yuma, or their preferred name the Euqchan) failed to materialize, the Quechan revolted against the Spanish and both missions and surrounding dwellings were destroyed on July 17, 1781. Through the following years beaver fur trappers passed through the area, but it was not until the end of the Mexican War in 1848, and the Gadsden Purchase in 1854, when the borders were redefined, that a true settlement was established at Yuma Crossing.

With the California gold rush in 1848 the crossing at Yuma became very significant so Fort Yuma was established in 1849. Yuma was popular because it was the only place to cross the Colorado River easily south of the Grand Canyon. The town on the Arizona side of the river became known as Colorado City at first but was changed to Arizona City in 1858. Over the next fifteen years the name changed back and forth between Yuma and Arizona City until permanently set as Yuma in 1873. While the Colorado River provided opportunities for Yuma through its steamboat stops, ferry crossings, and the rich soil surrounding the River, it also had several major floods, which devastated the town in 1852, 1890, 1905, 1916 and 1920.

After the flood of 1852 the town was re-built on higher ground. In 1876 a territorial prison was built in Yuma, in part because two legislators believed that locating the prison in Yuma would be a boost to the local economy. But Yuma was also an isolated town in a harsh environment, a fitting spot for punishment

The design of the prison was not the result of the work of an architect. To save money a contest was held and the winner received $150.00 for the plan of the prison. The prison was built on a hill, surrounded by the Gila River to the east, the Colorado River to the north, the city of Yuma to the west, and the open desert to the south. Surely such a location would discourage escape by its prisoners. Although one hundred and forty prisoners would attempt to escape, only twenty-six were successful, and of these only two escaped from within the prison itself. The other twenty-four escaped while working outside of the prison walls.

The prison was constructed mostly by prisoners themselves, perhaps a cruel addition to their sentences. You might imagine how they felt hauling and lifting the granite stones and the strap iron that would lock them away. On July 1, 1876 the first seven inmates moved into the new prison. Construction was ongoing and continued for the entire thirty-three years that the prison operated. The prison ended up having a kitchen, bakery, bathing room, library, and photo gallery. In 1885 a generator provided the prison with electricity at a time when much of the town did not have power. Eventually an agreement was made between prison officials and the Yuma Light and Power Company that after nine o'clock at night the prison would supply the power company with electricity. In return the Power Company provided the prison reservoir a continual supply of fresh water. In later years large blowers were installed which helped to cool the hot air in the prison cells. Because of the electricity, library, and fresh water, luxuries not available to a large portion of Yuma's population, the prison was often referred to as "The Country Club of the Colorado." Certainly today, the prison does not seem hospitable, but at the time it was a model institution.

A total of 3,069 prisoners were held at the prison during its thirty-three years of operation, including thirty-nine women. Despite being referred to as a country club, life inside the walls of Yuma Territorial Prison was brutal and harsh. Six prisoners were crowded into a narrow cell that contained two sets of triple bunk beds with only about two feet between them. The chamber pot for six was dumped only once a day. The cells also had an iron ring on the floor, used to attach a ball and chain to confine the prisoners for punishment. The beds were originally made of wood, but because the prisoners had serious problems with bedbugs, they were eventually changed to iron. Especially in the summer, the cells were virtually small furnaces, crowded with sweating prisoners, crawling with vermin, and stinking with human waste. Double sets of iron doors clanged tight insuring that no prisoner could escape their cells. Indeed the only two successful escapes from within the prison occurred from the New Yard, which was a large outside exercise area. During the years the prison was in operation one hundred and eleven prisoners died during their incarceration. While the causes of death varied, including attempted escape, suicide, and rattlesnake bite, disease was the most common cause of death. One third of all deaths at the Yuma Territorial Prison were from tuberculosis alone. Other diseases that spread through the prison were typhus, scarlet fever, and smallpox. Many of the prisoners who died are buried at the prison cemetery, which can still be visited today to the east of the prison.

The Yuma Territorial Prison closed its doors, due to overcrowding, on September 15, 1909 when a new prison in Florence, Arizona was opened. From 1910 to 1914 Yuma Union High School Students attended classes at the old prison hospital. After the flood of 1916, locals helped themselves to the free building materials available at the prison to rebuild the town, leading to the partial destruction of the prison. During the Great Depression, homeless people used the empty prison as a shelter. In the early 1940s, the people of Yuma converted the abandoned prison into a museum, and in 1961 it opened as an Arizona State Park. Today visitors can tour the cellblocks, the yards, the Dark Cell, the library, and the Guard Tower, which still stands, watching over the Yuma Territorial Prison and prisoners who may still roam the grounds.

Jesse Torres, Manager of the Yuma Territorial Prison, has worked at the site on and off since 1975. He has had one ghostly experience while working at the park, which occurred one morning before the park was open and he was in the museum. At the time the museum also functioned as the visitor center. He heard voices coming from the back offices and thought it was one of the other staff members. He describes the event as follows; "I said Linda are you here? Or I forget exactly what it was I said, and she answered. And then I walked outside, and I saw her standing outside, and I was like, wait a minute, that can't be true. So I went back inside and checked the office to see if there was somebody there and there wasn't anyone."

The museum building was originally the mess hall, and one can imagine a ghostly shadow answering Mr. Torres' question. However, his explanation for this oddity is somewhat more mundane. He says that from the way the building is constructed it is possible voices carry off the street, and when he asked the question, someone just happened to be talking down below. This is a possible explanation, but it is not the only odd occurrence in this building.

Linda Offeney has worked at the prison for twenty-two years, and used to take the admissions in the museum, until the admission desk was moved to the visitor center about three years ago. During the entire eighteen years she worked in the museum building she would regularly have problems with the cash register. Ms. Offeney explains what occurred in the building, "Every once in awhile we would have a ghost that we laughingly referred to as Johnny. Referring to Johnny Yuma, the TV show. And when I would go to the cash register to put nickels in the cash register they would try to jump out, or I would be a nickel off. They kind of just jumped out to the floor." This strange activity of jumping nickels happened intermittently. Sometimes Johnny showed up several times a month and then he would be quiet for six months or so. Since they started taking admissions in the visitor's center in 2003, it has been quiet. Perhaps the ghost Johnny, who would play games with Linda at the cash register, was the person who answered Jesse.

Cell 14 is the farthest cell on the left hand side of the picture.

Jumping coins and discarnate voices are not the only strange occurrences reported at the Yuma Territorial Prison. Cell 14 is reputed to be haunted as well. One of the prisoners in this cell was John Ryan and he was imprisoned for what was called a crime against nature, a sexual deviation offence. He was disliked by the other convicts and by the guards. On May 6, 1903 he used his bed sheets to hang himself in Cell 14. Visitors report they feel a presence or a change in temperature when they walk by that cell. In the end, John Ryan's only freedom was in the cold arms of death. Perhaps he still hangs high in his cell with the sheets yanked tightly around his neck. Going by you might catch an icy breath from this cell of loneliness.

Another story centers on the prison's Dark Cell. The Dark Cell was a notorious punishment cell within the prison. The cell, dug into the caliche hillside, is a room fifteen feet by fifteen feet. When sent to the Dark Cell for punishment, prisoners would be locked inside an iron cage, and their only light would come from a small ventilation shaft in the ceiling. Prisoners would be stripped out of their uniforms down to their undergarments, and given bread and water once a day. There are stories of guards dropping snakes and scorpions onto prisoners in the Dark Cell through the ventilation shaft, although these stories have not been confirmed.

Jesse Torres explains, "This prison had been abandoned for numerous years, and during the Great Depression a number of people started living in the cells. And one of the families that lived in the Dark Cell had a little girl, and she had a doll that had a red dress. Supposedly she was down by the river playing with her doll. Her doll falls into the water and she tries to retrieve it and drowns. So supposedly her spirit haunts the Dark Cell and she is attracted to anyone wearing red. She will reach out and pinch them and stuff like that."

During my visit to Yuma Territorial Prison, I was struck by how quiet, peaceful, and still the entire site felt, despite the numerous visitors milling about and its proximity to a railway. When I first entered the cell yard, it was empty of other visitors, and I could walk in peace to get a good sense of the place. As I approached the Dark Cell, I felt some fear and foreboding, but decided I would enter it anyway. It is like entering a dark cave. I tried to go in but the air became heavy and constricted, and I could not cross the threshold. I actually ran away from the cell and waited awhile until there were more people around. I then had my husband enter, he seemed to find no problems with the cell, so I tried to step in, but again felt a strong sense that I needed to leave. Perhaps because there is so little ventilation I was just feeling the effects of stale air, but it seemed like an unhappy place. The author of *Haunts of Arizona*, D. R. Kiefer, spent thirteen hours locked up during the night in the Dark Cell, and saw white shapes floating around him. Were these the spirits of the prisoners who were forced to endure hard times and terrible punishments in the Dark Cell? Was it the spirit of the little girl, looking for her doll, trying to ask for help? We will never know.

Several local ghost-hunting groups have made visits to

the Yuma Territorial Prison and they have found evidence of haunting at the prison. One group recently dubbed the New Yard a hot spot for activity. Since the New Yard is where two prisoners did manage to escape, it does not seem so strange that it would be home to some restless spirits. In fact, Jesse Torres did have one strange experience in the New Yard. He explains, "Well, as a kid I grew up here in Yuma. And our school group came here one day. And I could have sworn that I saw a shape of a convict in one of the cells in the New Yard." Overall though, Mr. Torres states that basically he doesn't believe in ghosts, and if he did he would not be working at the Yuma Territorial Prison.

While you are in Yuma visiting the Territorial Prison consider staying at the Historic Hotel Lee, the oldest hotel in Yuma. The hotel, in historic downtown Yuma, was built in 1917 in the Spanish Colonial Revival Style. Today the hotel has been restored and is on the National Register of Historic Places. Besides enjoying the great location of the hotel, and the historic feel, you might experience a ghost or three. Apparently three female ghosts haunt the halls of this historic hotel. The most commonly seen of these spirits is the hotel's original owner, who has been seen floating around the halls of the hotel and heard knocking on doors. Perhaps she has some unfinished business needing her attention, like a room to clean, or guests to wake up.

A visit to the Yuma Territorial Prison will tell you what it was like serving time in the old Southwest. The museum is full of artifacts and interpretative displays. The old cellblocks will give you pause. Perhaps when you visit the Dark Cell, you too will feel a dark foreboding presence and a heaviness set itself around you. Passing by Cell 14, you might shiver as the temperature drops suddenly and you sense a sad, despairing soul, eternally imprisoned. Wear red, and perhaps the cold, wet, small fingers of the poor little girl will reach out to touch you from the Dark Cell. It is a fact that when you visit the Yuma Territorial Prison, you cannot help but feel you have been touched by the past.

The former Pioneer Hotel

12

Tucson
This Old Pueblo is Haunted

Tucson, Arizona is an unusual city. It is a modern glittering city with over one million people, high tech industries, and a renowned university, yet Tucson preserves the enchantment of its frontier spirit and its desert past. Just one hundred miles away from Phoenix, it boasts a large and growing downtown, milder weather than Phoenix, along with several well preserved historic buildings. In this lovely and stately city, you can still find around virtually every corner the influence of Spain and old Mexico from long ago. What's more, as you explore Tucson, you might be asked for spare change by a man from the 30's, or hear hoof-beats where there are no horses now, or hear the muffled whispers of a ghostly audience in an empty theater. For Tucson, known as the "Old Pueblo", is irrevocably tied to its past.

Some say there are two Tucsons; the modern city of bright towers and highways and the old town still part of the desert, still troubled by past residents. This "Old Pueblo" will be here forever it seems; it has the patience of the ages, and for its departed residents the modern city is a mere mirage. There is something in Tucson that draws people here and makes it impossible for some of them to move elsewhere, even if it means a long commute into Phoenix for work. This tie that binds inhabitants here may last forever, for Tucson is an old haunted city.

The first residents of Tucson were likely Paleo-Indians, who hunted mammoth and bison in the area between 12,500 and 6,000 B.C. Then there was the Cochise culture, building pit houses and using stone tools. Later the Hohokum people lived in the area farming the fertile lands. Remains of their pit houses date back to 800-900 A.D. The name Tucson itself is from the Pima word *schookson* or *stjukshon*, which means "at the foot of the dark mountain." It is believed that this mountain refers to Sentinel Mountain, today known as "A Mountain" thanks to the large letter "A" originally made with white-washed stones (in early 2008 it was green) on the mountain by a group of students from the University of Arizona.

In 1691 Father Eusebio Francisco Kino arrived in Arizona to carry out missionary work for the Jesuits. He choose a small Pima village in 1694 to be a visita (a clerical outpost of his missionary), and called it San Augustín de Oiaur; another Pima village a short distance away he called San Cosme de Tucson. Eventually the entire area became known as Tucson.

In 1775 a site was selected near the present day courthouse in Tucson for the construction of a Spanish Presidio (a military garrison). The Spanish Empire built several Presidios near their northern border and near Apache strongholds. In 1786 the Spanish introduced the Gálvez Plan, which established trading posts among the tribes in the area. The plan, which was put in place after signing treaties, was a way to pacify the Apaches with access to food, alcohol, and guns. But in the 1830s the Mexican government stopped the amenities that were offered under this plan and warfare resumed. The Mexican government felt it had other things to worry about closer to home, and the Gálvez plan was expensive. In the 1840s Tucson was still a small village, remaining part of Mexico until 1853 when it was acquired during the Gadsden Purchase. The impressions of outsiders were not always favorable of this walled rowdy adobe village. It was known for its casinos and playhouses, and men went about the town well armed at all times.

While Tucson was a little behind the times, and in many ways was more of a Mexican Pueblo than an American city, in the later 1800s it became more linked to the outside world. In 1870 the telegraph arrived and in the 1880s the telephone, gas streetlights, and the Southern Pacific Railroad finally reached Tucson. After this the city industrialized and became the second largest city in Arizona. Today, Tucson is a modern city, although there are many areas where the Old Pueblo still exists, and where ghosts still roam.

The Sosa-Carrillo-Frémont House Museum is a must see location for those wanting a flavor of old Tucson. This house has a long history relating to some of the most prominent of Tucson residents. Manuela Sosa and Michael McKenna originally owned the property on which the current house stands. They inherited the property from José María Sosa III, the first person to have owned the land. Jesusita Suárez de Carrillo purchased the Sosa house in 1878; she died in 1880. Her husband Leopoldo completed the house around 1880-1881 using components of the Sosa house that stood on the site. In 1881, the completed house was rented to John C. Frémont, who was known as the "Pathfinder" for his exploration and mapping of the Oregon Trail. He was also the Fifth Territorial Governor of Arizona. While Frémont rented the house, it is unlikely that he ever lived there, but his daughter, Elizabeth lived there in 1881. After Elizabeth left, the Carrillo family moved into the home and lived there for the next ninety years; some say they have never left.

These three prominent families gave the Sosa-Carrillo-Frémont House its name. In 1967, plans were underway to build the Tucson Convention Center in the neighborhood where the Sosa-Carrillo-Frémont House stands. As many as 250 homes and businesses were slated to be demolished. Luckily, the Tucson Heritage Foundation recognized the importance of the home, and it was saved from destruction. In 1971 the Arizona

Historical Society purchased and restored the home, and it was soon opened to the public. The house is on the National Register of Historic Places. Ironically it was principally the tenuous association with John Frémont that saved the house, not the long association with one of Tucson's most prominent families (the Carrillo's), or the architectural significance of the house.

The Sosa-Carrillo-Frémont House is a typical Mexican residential house. Upon entering the house you are in the *zaguán*, a long hallway from one end of the house to the other. All other rooms open into the *zaguán*, and because there are doors on each end, the cross breezes often make it the most comfortable part of the house.

In the *zaguán* a large diamond dust mirror is on display.

149

This mirror was a Carrillo family piece. Jesusita Carrillo died in 1880, leaving behind nine children. Leopoldo eventually married her sister Elvira Saurez who was already taking care of the children; the marriage was needed because it otherwise would have been improper for them to live together. It is believed that Elvira is one of the ghosts that walks the halls and drifts through the rooms at the Sosa-Carrillo-Frémont House. A woman is seen frequently at the large mirror, bent over as if in great pain, holding her stomach, while holding onto the mirror for support. It is not widely known, but Elvira died of stomach cancer, so it seems likely this is her ghostly image gently weeping, holding onto a favorite possession for support. A woman's figure has also been seen in the back of the house walking towards the kitchen. Perhaps Elvira relives fonder events as well in her former home.

A male figure is also seen in the Sosa-Carrillo-Frémont House and this is believed to be Leopoldo Carrillo. Leopoldo was a very wealthy man when he lived in Tucson, and as such built himself a very fine home. In 1881 it is reported that he owned over one hundred buildings in Tucson. He also brought many luxuries to the people of Tucson. Leopoldo built the first public park in Tucson in 1885, called Carrillo's Gardens. These gardens had fruit trees and ponds where the public could enjoy boat rides. There was also a zoo, a circus, a saloon, bathhouses, restaurants, and a dance hall. He also built a small private school on the grounds. Leopoldo also brought to Tucson the first bowling alley, the first ice cream parlor, constructed the first two-story building, and was the first to use wooden floors.

Leopoldo died when he was only 54 years old. Perhaps he is relaxing now and enjoying with pride his wonderful home. He can be seen walking on the wood floors, the first of their kind in Tucson. At other times, he can be seen sitting in the living room, enjoying the musical instruments in the room.

The earliest residents of the house also make their presence felt. In the Sosa bedroom the sounds of teenagers laughing has been heard. This room lies on the foundation of the former Sosa house, and the McKenna girls (Catherine and Manuela, daughters of Manuela Sosa and Michael McKenna) might be revisiting their former home.

The ghostly presences in the house seem kind and happy, except perhaps Elvira. When they are not seen, they are felt in other ways. Sometimes the motion detector will get tripped in the middle of the night, but upon inquiry, there is nobody in the house. Doors open and close on their own and footsteps are heard echoing on the floors when no one is present. The Carrillo family ghosts are friendly and seem content to have their home open to the public.

The Sosa-Carrillo-Frémont House is not the only haunted locale in Tucson. This town is so haunted it even features its own ghost tour. Several of the haunted locations are in the downtown area, including the Fox Tucson Theatre. The Fox Theatre opened its doors on April 11, 1930 as a vaudeville/ movie house. That night Tucson had the biggest party in its history as the town came alive to see this new movie palace.

For the next forty-four years the Fox Theatre entertained the people of Tucson with live shows and movies, until competition from television and drive-ins, and the decline in the downtown, forced this once magnificent movie palace to close. In 2000 the theatre was bought by the Fox Tucson Theatre Foundation and they undertook an extensive thirteen million dollar renovation of the building. The theatre is now on the National Register of Historic Places and re-opened to the public on December 31, 2005.

Today the visiting public can relive the Fox Theatre's past with a mix of movies, high-definition telecasts of concerts, and live performances. While there is an old adage that every theatre needs at least one ghost, the story of the ghost of the Fox Theatre relates to the exterior of the building. A man dressed in clothes from the 1930s can be seen hovering around the box office of this theatre. He will ask passersby for money to feed his family, who are desperate and suffering from the Great Depression. While he seems to be a solid figure, his old-fashioned garb always sets people aback. After hearing his plea, his figure fades into the night, another ghost of old Tucson.

A short walk away from the Fox Theatre is the former Pioneer Hotel, (now an office building), which was the scene of the worst fire in Tucson's history. It was December 20, 1970 and 350 employees from the Hughes Aircraft Company were celebrating in the ballroom. Hotel rooms were full of sleeping guests, recovering from a long day of shopping. At 12:19 a.m., the fire department received the first of three calls, "fire at the Pioneer Hotel." It seemed like a hoax, since many false alarms were called in from the hotel over the years. The ballroom, which had highly flammable carpeting, wallpaper, and Christmas decorations, quickly caught fire and the fire spread rapidly throughout the hotel. Guests staying in the upper floors died in their sleep or while trying to escape the flames by jumping from the windows. When the fire department did arrive, their ladders did not reach the upper stories of the hotel. In all twenty-nine people died that night in the fire at the Pioneer Hotel, which is believed to have been caused by arson. This tragedy did have some positive effects in that it caused significant building code changes, including requirements for smoke detectors and sprinklers in buildings over four stories high, non-flammable carpeting, and ladders on fire trucks able to reach the tallest floors of the buildings.

With so much suffering and tragedy at the Pioneer Hotel that dark day in December 1970, it is not so strange echoes of that night still remain. Today employees in the new Pioneer Office Building say they smell acrid smoke when there is no worldly source. They also hear frantic cries and running on the upper floors, as the victims of the fire relive their tragic end over and over again into eternity.

If your travels to Tucson involve staying overnight, the best choice for your stay is the historic Hotel Congress. The Hotel Congress is conveniently located in downtown Tucson, within walking distance of all the haunted locales already discussed, and haunted in its own right.

The Hotel Congress opened its doors in 1919, with its ideal location across the road from the train station that served passengers on the Southern Pacific Line. On January 22, 1934 a fire broke out in the basement of the Congress and quickly spread to the third floor of the hotel. This fire eventually destroyed the third floor; it is the story of some occupants of the third story during the fire that is of interest. For some of John Dillinger's (one of the most notorious criminals in the country) gang were staying at the hotel under aliases. They escaped the fire, but desperately pleaded with the firemen to retrieve their luggage. The heavy bags contained $23,816 in cash, and many weapons. Later realizing who the men were, a stakeout occurred on a house on North Second Avenue, and the whole gang was captured. The downfall of the famous bank robber John Dillinger is directly related to the fire at the Hotel Congress.

This charming hotel still has its original switchboard, old lobby fixtures, and a restful relaxing feeling. An odd family of ghosts has been unable to leave this hotel, but I was assured they are all good spirits. On the second floor a man dressed in an old-fashioned grey suit has been seen peering out of the windows. It is believed he may have died in a gunfight over a card game, and he is known as T.S. A female spirit has been seen in the lobby and on the stairwell. She is always in a long dress and brings a scent of roses. Perhaps she is a former guest that enjoyed her time so thoroughly at the Hotel Congress that she never left. I was also told that a little girl spirit is active in the hotel. She can be seen flittering around hallways, laughing softly, and playfully opening and closing doors.

Hotel Congress

One of the most recent additions to the ghostly repertoire at the Hotel Congress is Vince. In 1954 a man named Vince arrived in Tucson on the railway, exited the station, and came over to the Hotel Congress. He never left, working there until he died in 2001. The housekeepers of the hotel see, feel, and sense him all the time. Hotel staff find butter knives all over the second floor. Vince used to use butter knives as screwdrivers. Perhaps he has never really left his work behind? On the day of my visit, I was told that a housekeeper had experienced an encounter with Vince that very morning, and could smell his presence.

Centennial Hall on the University of Arizona Campus also is reputed to harbor ghosts. The Hall was designed by

Roy Place, a prominent Tucson architect, and constructed in 1936. It is the University's largest performance venue, seating approximately 2,450 patrons. Place used red brick for the Hall and now red brick facades are a prominent feature of many of the University buildings. At least two spirits are reputed to haunt the building, nicknamed Herman and Matilda by custodial staff. Herman is said to be tall, thin and always dressed in black. He seems young with short brown hair and he is very elusive, he appears and then vanishes in a wink. Perhaps he was a stage hand as he is seen on or near the stage and once on the catwalk. But Matilda is even more evasive; she is only glimpsed vaguely. She is said to appear in a long evening gown of blue or green, which seems to catch the wind like chiffon. Perhaps she was an artist or maybe a patron. Some say they have heard weeping and wonder if this is Matilda, forever trapped in the Hall. Other strange phenomena witnessed include horse hoof-beats echoing from the street throughout the theater, perhaps from patrons arriving decades ago, and vacuum cleaners running themselves. The sound of a piano is sometimes heard late at night. You can imagine a long dead artist dreamily performing to an audience of lonely lost spirits. There are wraiths in Centennial Hall; quiet conversations sound from empty rooms, footfalls echo in empty halls. While there be aware of shadowy movements on the stage – it may be Herman, and listen for soft crying, perhaps Matilda is coming to you for comfort.

Tucson, Arizona has come a long way from the tiny Pueblo so far away from anything, so slow to have any modern changes or conveniences. Today, Tucson is a booming metropolis, but this old Pueblo has not forgotten its past. As you approach on the busy freeway the swirling dust in the desert might not be just the wind but the lingering smoke of encampments of ages ago, for this city is surrounded by its past. The desert roots are deep and everlasting in Tucson. And in the city the past remains, perhaps in fragments and in ruins but in a sense more permanent and lasting than the modern, towering glass buildings which to the hosts of the dead are nothing but mirages. Tucson is alive with ghosts, who have time forever.

Interior of the Tumacácori Mission Church

13

Tumacácori National Historic Park
A Congregation of the Departed

As you walk through the arched entrance into the Tumacácori Mission Church you feel a calmness descend upon you. Here serenity overcomes you as you rest in the garden and wander through the church ruins. There is a feeling that this is a place where you would like to stay forever. It is as if guardian angels surround you. Perhaps this feeling is shared by three priests, who are so devoted to their work they are said to tend the mission gardens still and celebrate mass to an ethereal congregation long after their deaths. These Tumacácori ruins are in the Mesquite highlands a short distance north of the Mexican border. The area around the ruins is remote, the only close town,

Tubac, a mere two miles away is a small artists' retreat and the rugged Sierrita Mountains loom in the distance.

Over five hundred years ago, the O'odham people lived along the San Pedro and Santa Cruz rivers. Their first contact with Europeans was in 1540 when the Spanish explorer Francisco Vázquez de Coronado crossed over what is now southeastern Arizona. He and his conquistadors were searching for mythical cities of gold, and were uninterested in the tiny villages of the O'odham (or Pima as they called them) and left them alone. The O'odham continued to live a peaceful existence without conflict with the Spanish for many years.

In 1691 Father Eusebio Francisco Kino and Father Visitor Salvatierra arrived at Tumacácori. At the time Tumacácori was a small town with around forty houses. Father Kino and Father Salvatierra baptized the children in town, held a mass, and moved on. Tumacácori was the first mission established in what is today Arizona. The next day at Guevavi (fifteen miles upriver from Tumacácori) their local headquarters was established and the building of the first church started. While Father Kino wanted permanent missionaries at Tumacácori as well, he made due with visits as often as he or another priest could make the trip. It was not until the mid 1700s that the first church was built at Tumacácori.

In 1751 two priests and more than one hundred settlers were killed during a Pima revolt at Tumacácori. Because of this revolt, a presidio was built in nearby Tubac, and Tumacácori was moved to the west side of the river in 1753. The new missionary built a small church in 1757, and in 1771 the mission headquarters were moved from Guevavi to Tumacácori. This church was destroyed during another raid, and building on another mission started in 1800, although lack of funds brought construction to a halt. Church construction resumed in 1821, but with Mexican Independence, Spain withdrew its support, and work on the mission ceased.

In 1828 Mexico ordered Spanish born priests to leave the country, after which time there was never a resident priest at Tumacácori. In 1844 Tumacácori's land was declared abandoned (despite the settlers who remained) by the Mexican authorities. Finally Tumacácori was completely abandoned in 1848 because of continuing Apache attacks, a harsh winter, and the Mexican-American War. The soldiers left Tubac, and the last residents left Tumacácori taking the church's statues, chalices, and vestments to San Xavier del Bac (near Tucson) for safekeeping. It is the ruins of the church which can be seen today at Tumacácori National Historic Park; the site was declared a National Monument in 1908.

A visit to Tumacácori National Historic Park begins in the Visitors' Center where you can learn about the other local missions, including Guevavi and Calabazas. Further exhibit rooms and a video tell of life of the O'odham people living on this mission. Once you exit the museum you enter into the park and can view the church and the foundation ruins of the O'odham houses.

Built out of sun-dried adobe bricks the church is

about fifty feet wide by one hundred feet long. The walls are substantial, ranging from five to ten feet thick. There is a wonderful entrance - arched and framed by double columns. Originally, the exterior walls of the church were brightly painted, a small portion of which can still be seen today; there is a faint hue of rose or salmon on many exterior walls. The columns were painted red and the capitals crowning the columns were painted yellow and black; this paintwork is reminiscent in a strange way of Egyptian architecture. The interior of the church was even more colorful and remnants of the beautifully painted walls can still be seen.

Tumacácori Mission Church

Inside the church there are no pews, as people stood or knelt during the services. The nave is a long hall and is not in the shape of a cross due to lack of funds (it was part of the original plan to have the church in the shape of a cross). How many former celebrants, penitents and grievers have passed away, yet left traces of their feet and knees on the hard floor and traces of their fingers on the ruins of the holy water fonts? This is a holy place. If you listen on a quiet evening, can you hear the choir praising God? Perhaps at night phantom votive candles flicker in a rush of cool night desert air.

The roof of the bell tower was never built. Under the altar steps two priests, who helped to build the church, are buried. When the church was abandoned in 1848 the roof was removed (likely by local settlers for use as building materials). The roof was replaced in 1921, 1947, and 1978, but the nave was still exposed for over sixty years, which has caused a lot of damage. Still much remains and a visitor can get a real sense of what it was like inside this church for the O'odham people. You also gather a feeling of peace in the church, there is a sense of the sacred here. At first there is a musty smell of old dust upon entering the church but then, it seems more like vanilla and sandalwood or incense drifting from years ago.

While it is said the last residents abandoned Tumacácori in 1848, perhaps some of them linger still, as there have been ghostly echoes around Tumacácori since the late 1800s. A story of what a few cowboys saw while traveling through the area, herding cattle, was recounted in the Arizona Daily Star in 1882. Henry Perkins and his companions were so worn out that they could not make it to Tubac, so they decided to spend the night in the ruins of Tumacácori. At the time there was no roof over the building, so the moonlight streamed in and they built a small fire inside the nave for warmth. Exhausted, the men soon fell asleep wrapped in their saddle blankets. This sleep was short lived as they were all startled awake together, as if stung by scorpions. Before them a strange purple light glowed in front of the altar. From this came a chanting sound, and slowly the image of a priest with an acolyte (altar server) on either side of him formed out of the mist. The chanting continued and the priest turned towards the men and said something that sounded like a prayer. When the priest turned back towards the altar and knelt again, the entire church seemed to fill up with smoky and shadowy human forms, kneeling on the floor. The priest chanted louder and the spectral congregation knelt lower and then seemed to dissolve into the floor, as the chanting suddenly ceased. These cattle-drive-toughened cowboys collapsed shaking and afraid from what they had witnessed. They prayed for the dawn. This rich visitation may have been sparked by the ranch hands desecration of the holy space.

The spirits of Fathers Baltazar, Carillo, and Narcisco Guiterres are believed to appear at the ruins of Tumacácori every year during the Festival of San Juan. This festival celebrates the arrival of the Summer Solstice and the longest day of the year from June 20th-24th. These three priests have been seen working in the mission garden and orchards over the years by many local people. They have also been seen at night ringing the bells in the bell tower and holding services for their phantom parishioners. The priests have been able to bring back together their flock, scattered by death, to worship forever in this old church, which seems to be held in the hands of serenity.

While you are at Tumacácori take a side trip to Tubac and visit this old town, Arizona's oldest European community. There is the Anza trail, which runs about 4.5 miles along the Santa Cruz River from Tumacácori to Tubac. But you will find shade from mesquite, hackberry, cottonwood, and willow trees and you may catch sight of vermillion flycatchers or red-winged blackbirds or Gila woodpeckers. Tubac was established in 1752 as a Spanish fort, and the ruins of this original fort can be seen today at the Tubac Presidio State Historic Park.

Tubac is well known to harbor a female ghost dressed in black. She wanders about this town, sometimes appearing outside of people's homes, materializing out of nowhere. Some residents believe it is buried treasure this woman is looking for. Gil Procter chronicled her appearances in the Tubac Bugle in 1965 and 1966; as has Lorraine Casanega Sholly in the Green Valley News in 1968. The Ghost of Tubac, as she is known, is said to always be dressed in black and is short at four feet tall. Black is for mourning so perhaps this woman is doomed to grieve forever in Tubac. Maybe you will see her, like a mist of black disappearing around a building, as you explore this old town, which is now an artist's colony.

A visit to Tumacácori State Historic Park and nearby Tubac will enlighten you on the early history of the southern part of Arizona when it was under Spanish rule. The ruins will inspire you and the site will let you see what life was like for O'odham people who lived near the Tumacácori mission. While marveling at the beauty and stillness of the ruins, marvel also at the eternal mass celebrated here by the spirits of priests forever serving their parish. Perhaps you will hear a faint chant from the choir loft or catch the scent of water and wine or maybe, outside the church you will see a man dressed in a white, cotton surplice. In Tubac, that woman walking in front of you dressed in a long black dress, strangely old-fashioned, may suddenly vanish around a corner. If so, count yourself with good fortune, you have been blessed with a vision.

14

Gammons Gulch Ghost Town
Phantoms from Afar

Near the rolling hills of Benson, Arizona lies the ghost town of Gammons Gulch. This ghost town is a remarkable assemblage of buildings and artifacts from all over Arizona. Film crews use the saloon, blacksmith's shop, jail, hotel, and other buildings as the perfect backdrop for music videos and movies. Though created, Gammons Gulch rings true. Visitors feel they have been transported back to the days of the Wild West. This ambiance of authenticity is confirmed by the presence of several ghosts who seem attached to particular objects. Strangely, these visitors from beyond appear either to find solace and comfort in objects, like a toddler with a blanket, or deliver malice from apparently inanimate objects. Arizona ghosts are not mere shadows of imagination or mirages of the desert sun. Many seem to be replaying their lives oblivious to the living.

Jay Gammons had always wanted to build a Ghost Town. Thirty-five years ago, he drove by the land where Gammons Gulch sits today and noticed a sign advertising ten acres for five thousand dollars. Jay liked the location, the land was inexpensive, and so his labor of love began. Little did he know of the land's troubled history when he bought it. Years ago, just south of Gammons Gulch and just north of Benson was a stagecoach station called the San Pedros Station, later changed to Ohnesorgen Station. During the Apache wars from 1861-1886, this stagecoach station was used as a fort. An Apache tribe near Gammons Gulch used the peaks just beyond the town as lookout points. When you reach the mountain tops on the property you can see for miles. In the past, there was also a small stream running by the land; today the land is dry and bare; you are in the high desert country of Cochise County.

Around the movie set town, cactus and tumbleweeds dot the landscape creating a picture of what we imagine a Ghost Town should look like. Be aware however; the tumbleweeds rumbling towards you may be the dry fragments of the Apache, still fighting desperately for their homeland. Let them continue their roaming. This high desert was their home for ages and now they are gone and only their spirits ride the lonely winds here.

Today, Jay and his wife Joanne live at Gammons Gulch

in the hotel building, along with the ghosts. The curious part of the ghostly activity at Gammons Gulch is that the town is not old. The buildings are made from reclaimed building materials or relocated from other towns from around Arizona. As Jay takes you on a tour through town he can name where every door and beam came from. The mercantile was a house in Benson, dating to 1893, the flooring in the jail came from a building dating to 1896, and the door at the back of the jail came from Tombstone. The hotel is a modern building that Jay constructed, but it contains beams from the ghost town of Ruby. There is even a beam from the Good Enough Mine in Tombstone inside the Gammons Gulch mine.

Within all of these buildings are numerous antiques with a wide variety of origins. The site also has an impressive collection of antique cars. Attached to all of these antiques and old buildings, there are more than mere legends and campfire stories; there are lingering spirits in this lonely town. Joanne explains, "I think anyone who knows anything about ghosts, knows that sometimes they will go with an article, a piece of furniture, a picture. They can carry on with almost anything, and this town is full of possibilities from one end to the other." Are the inanimate objects and buildings of Gammons Gulch really alive with spirits? The answer appears to be yes. Most ghosts appear to be chained to a particular locale, but not all, as some seem to be able to escape and take their haunting afar.

Joanne explains that her first experience with anything strange was when she first came to the town in 1992. At that time, the hotel was set up like an old Wild West hotel. In the lobby of the hotel was an old pew from a church in Benson that had a fire, which damaged but did not destroy the building. Joanne states that every time she went into the lobby it was ice cold. Keep in mind this is Arizona, and nothing is ice cold any time of the year. She says the whole room was disturbing and she did not like the feeling in there. As she suspected the church pew was the source of malice, it needed to go. Joanne is unsure what exactly it was about the church pew that was so uninviting, but she knew somehow that the sense of uneasiness was caused by that church pew. They found an antiques dealer in Tombstone, who traded a barbershop chair for the church pew. Once the church pew was gone, the eerie coldness and the negative gloomy mood of the room departed.

Gammons Gulch Hotel

The interesting follow up to this story is that the antique dealer was never able to sell the church pew. Nobody wanted anything to do with it. After he acquired the church pew, his business began to suffer and eventually he had to sell out and moved to Indiana. At the auction to sell off the remaining antiques from his business, the church pew still did not sell, and has remained in the building. And to this day, whatever business goes into this space fails and now even the building is taboo as it cannot attract buyers. Some objects seem to harbor malice and spread dread and despair throughout their surroundings. This appears true for the haunted church pew.

Even with the church pew gone, all was not quiet with the hotel. Another spirit, a lady, calls this space her home. A caretaker who lived at the property when Joanne first came to town, told her to be careful about going upstairs in the hotel. Joanne states, "She said there is something there, I don't know what it is, I just know there is something there." This caretaker did see a lady upstairs, and for some reason this spirit likes the stairwell in the house. One day the caretaker was pushed at the top of the stairs, she fell, feet first, down the first three steps. Another time, there was a movie crew on-site and one of the young men on the crew was being disrespectful in the hotel; later he too was pushed down the top three steps. One more visitor was also bumped down the stairs. Afterwards Joanne discovered that the visitor had been helping herself to a few things around the property. Joanne feels this phantom lady is a protector to her and Jay, and the shoving of people down the stairs is a warning. As Joanne says the lady's actions are really only a nudging of people on the stairs "never enough to hurt them, just enough to make them leery of doing anything."

One day Joanne spotted this lady in the hotel lobby. She describes the encounter, "I saw her personally one time. And it was nothing bad; it just happened that I saw her. She was down in the lobby, just an outline of her. A slender tall woman, dark hair, seems to have a long skirt on, but she has never done anything to Jay or I, nothing at all. She has been a good entity; she is like a protection here. I don't know where she came from; she was here before I got here. She might have come from something that Jay put there, something that was brought in prior to that time. But it is nothing bad, it is nothing bad."

Another spirit has also been seen on the property, across the street from the hotel, lingering near the well. Joanne is unsure if this is the same lady as the one inside the house, but thinks it is unlikely she would have ventured outside. This woman is described as medium height with long hair, but oddly she is seen wearing men's pants. It is not just Joanne who has been visited by these specters. A woman who does office work for the site has witnessed the woman in pants standing listlessly by the well and also saw the woman with the long wispy skirt in the hotel.

The last known ghost residing in the hotel is of a cat. Joanne said, "This started about two years ago. We have a cat, and seeing a cat around the house is not that unusual for me. I came out of my room, and looked and all of a sudden I saw a cat run across the floor. And I thought it was Shadow, my cat, and I look down, and Shadow is downstairs, and I thought I was seeing things. But it happened three more times. And it always happens this time of the year, [fall] and sometimes early spring. Early spring is probably the first time it showed itself to me. He is cute, he runs across the hall and runs to the bathroom or the other bedroom and he is gone. He is a Siamese, and it is like he is playing a little game with me. He runs up the steps, and down the hallway, and into the other bedroom or bathroom. I didn't say anything and then one day, I said to Jay did you have cats in here before I came along?" It turns out that Jay's mother's cat had lived there, he was Siamese, and his name was Chongo. He died in the hotel, but is not buried at the Pet Cemetery on the grounds of the town, as it did not exist at the time of his death.

Gammons Gulch Ghost Town

There is another spirit wandering the grounds of Gammons Gulch Ghost Town. He is a man, perhaps a miner, but he is always seen in front of the cemetery. Perhaps he died in a mine (perhaps the Good Enough Mine) and was never buried and is now condemned to wait at the gates of this cemetery forever. The Gammons are unsure if he is a miner or a caretaker, but he is described by visitors as a slender man wearing overalls. Beside the physical portrayal he is also said to watch visitors very intently, as if wondering why they do not help him. There is some thought that he might be associated with the beam that was taken from the Good Enough Mine in Tombstone. Joanne has not yet seen this man, but the woman who does office work for her has seen him, as have visitors. He was first spotted in 2003 and has made a few appearances since then.

If your travels in Arizona take you to the southeastern part of the state, it is worth a side trip to Gammons Gulch Ghost Town and Movie Set. While there, you will feel transported to the days of the Wild West. Perhaps the past will touch you in more ways than the old buildings overflowing with antiques. Perhaps you will see a ghostly woman with long dark hair, a slender man dressed in overalls searching for his resting place, or a cat seeking its former home.

15

Tombstone
Ghosts Too Tough to Die

Tombstone, Arizona creates images in almost everyone's mind of the classic old Wild West town. We can picture the saloons, bordellos, the wild gunfights, endless card games, and the lonely cemeteries. Today these come to life first hand for visitors who can watch recreated gunfights, trod the remade streets, and visit the reconstructed buildings that have become a legend unto themselves. Tombstone nearly became a ghost town when the mines closed down in 1936. But this town was too tough to die, too tough to suffer the same fate as countless other mining boomtowns. Now, Tombstone is reborn as a tourist attraction, bringing visitors back to the 1880s. Perhaps the reconstructions and restorations are too accurate, as rumors of ghosts and hauntings permeate this small town. Maybe the spirits decided that if this town is too tough to die, they are as well.

How does a town get a name like Tombstone? This unusual name came from Ed Schieffelin, who founded the town in 1877. While a solider at Fort Huachuca he prospected in the area around present day Tombstone trying to find his riches. This was no picnic as the area was inhabited by tribes of Apache who were not welcoming prospectors. The other soldiers joked with him that the only thing he would find in the area was his own tombstone. However, Schieffelin was determined, and lucky, for he struck a rich silver vein. Remembering the jokes made about his choice of location, he called his first claim Tombstone, and later the emerging boomtown took hold of this name.

The town was founded on a flat mesa, surrounded by the Whetstone, Mule, Burro, Huachuca, and Dragoon Mountains. Standing on the dirt of Allen Street, which is the original center of the rowdy town, sometimes you can feel the wind come down from the hills, high and lonesome, kicking up the dust and ashes of those who died long ago. Perhaps it's the specter of Wyatt Earp crossing the street, not an actor. Maybe it's not a painting of a madam behind a dirty window, but Dutch Annie winking and beckoning you. Beyond the veneer of the tourist attractions lives the true old Tombstone; now and then it flashes alive.

Together with his brother Al, Ed Schieffelin claimed seventeen mines around Tombstone. It was a rich mining district; from 1879 to 1936 the mines in the area produced $37,103,008 in silver ore and other minerals. All of the mining sites around Tombstone discovered by the Schieffelin brothers bore eccentric names including: Graveyard No. 1 and 2, Tough Nut, Good Enough, Owl's Nest, and Lucky Cuss.

While the mines founded the town of Tombstone, the bloody gunfights, gambling and drinking, and red light ladies made it famous. The most legendary of the gunfights was the shoot-out at the OK Corral. The accounts vary of this legendary episode of the old west. However, it seems the gun battle lasted about thirty seconds and thirty shots were fired. When the hail of bullets stopped three outlaws lay dead and either two or three of the lawmen injured as some reports say only Wyatt Earp escaped unharmed. The outlaws (Billy Clanton, Tom and Frank McLaury) faced the law (John "Doc" Holliday, Morgan Earp, Virgil Earp, and Wyatt Earp) in the battle. Ike Clanton and Bill Claibourne ran away from the fight, unharmed, although other accounts say Doc Holliday shot at Ike Clanton and perhaps wounded him. There has been a great deal of debate over the years about who fired the first shot. At the time, Doc Holliday and the Earp brothers were arrested, but witnesses at the preliminary hearing declared the Clantons and McLaury fired the first shots. Regardless of who started the battle it lives in southwestern legend.

The prospecting frenzy swelled the population of Tombstone quickly and by 1882 the town was home to 5,300 people. Later as many as 10,000 people lived in the area. With a growing population and the scent of money, Tombstone attracted a hoard of swindlers, rustlers, and thieves. Everyone wanted a piece of a new claim. Pimps and madams had hands deep into miners' pockets, shady lawyers drew up false claims, and cardsharps took all they could at the poker tables. The saloons had an endless supply of drink to loosen up the silver and gold sacks. Killers lurked in the shadowed alleys. This was a grueling time of struggle in Arizona as the sun was fierce and the high desert fraught with dangers. There was little water and the desert was full of rattlesnakes and scorpions. Apache warriors, whose lands, rich with silver and gold, were being stolen, fought for their families, for their ancestors, for their way of life.

Life was short for many so they lived hard. Violence was commonplace and in Tombstone the smell of blood often mingled with the smell of horses and leather on the streets. While in the bars, even the cigar smoke couldn't mask the musky perfume of the whores, who lusted after gold more than anything. It became a dangerous and lawless town but full of excitement. With so many people there was entertainment for all. Some of the best known entertainers of the day turned up in Tombstone. Beatrice Leo and her husband Jerry Hart, both actors, played the Bird Cage in 1882. Magician Charles (Uncle Charlie) Andress played in the 1880s. Ladies who graced the stage included Pearl Ardine, Ella Gardiner, Lola Cory, Annie Duncan, and Nola Forrest. While these names were famous in the 1880s, today they have mostly faded into oblivion.

The most famous spot in Tombstone was the Bird Cage

Theatre, which opened on December 23, 1881. It ran non-stop twenty-four hours a day, seven days a week, feeding the vices of Tombstone. During its heyday the theatre witnessed sixteen gunfights. You can still see the remnants of these bloody battles in the one hundred and forty bullet holes in the walls and ceiling of the Bird Cage Theatre. There were other dens of vice in Tombstone but the Bird Cage became the most popular. You could watch the shows while gambling, drinking, and enjoying the company of the women of the house. And if it touched your fancy you could just shoot off your Colt .45 for fun. But if someone cheated at cards, you would settle the score with some lead into his heart. The riotous living lasted while the mines did. In 1883, the mines flooded and the economy declined. The Bird Cage Theatre was sold and forced to close its doors for several months. Then in 1884 a miners' strike (the fourth one in Tombstone's history) and a bank failure destroyed the town's economy. But in 1886 the Bird Cage Theatre was reopened under the name The Elite and it stayed open until 1892 but was only a faded image of its glory days.

Today you still enter the Bird Cage Theatre through the bar. A staffer will regale you with stories of the shootouts, while you belly up to the original cherry wood bar and count the bullet holes riddling the walls. The nine foot tall portrait of Fatima, a notorious exotic dancer, has been hanging in the same spot right inside the entrance since 1882. Inside the theatre the original benches are long gone. Display cases exhibit memorabilia from the old days of the Bird Cage. The original business license issued by Cochise County in 1881 to Dutch Annie Smith to operate a "House of Ill Fame" hangs on the wall, and Doc Holliday's' faro table sits in the theatre. Faded red and blue curtains adorn the stage and the piano sits in its original spot at the foot of the stage. On each side of the theatre are seven suspended "birdcages" where ladies of the night would entertain their male clients, while they enjoyed the never-ending shows. Faded red velvet curtains drape the front of these rooms; the wallpaper is now faded and stained. On each side of the theatre two narrow staircases ascend to these cribs of sin, where the "soiled doves," the "tainted angels," the "painted birds" plied their trade. Today the birdcages are off limits to visitors, although you can get a very good view from the main floor.

Behind the stage curtain are more displays including the Black Mariah, an original hearse used in Tombstone's Wild West days to take the dead to Boothill Cemetery. Below the stage are the original dressing rooms, where the old stage garments still hang and you can imagine the performers preparing for the evening's events. This is also where you will see the poker tables and another bar. This is the site of an almost perpetual card game that lasted a staggering eight years, five months and three days, making it the longest card game in Western history. The stakes were high in this game as the table had a thousand dollar minimum. The chairs are said be in the exact position they were in when the game ended all those years ago. Just beyond the card tables under the stage are the old wine barrels which fueled the spending and fighting.

When the Bird Cage Theatre was closed in 1892 it was sealed for years. Literally, after the last night in business, the doors were shut and sealed. This was a Godsend, because when reopened the entire original fixtures were intact, even if they were well worn with the passage of years. This fortuitous preserving makes the Bird Cage unique in its old West treasures.

The Bird Cage was reopened as a theatre for the first Helldorado celebration in October 1929. This is a yearly event in Tombstone on the third weekend in October. Visitors can witness the old gunfights again and enjoy a carnival and a parade. In 1934 the Bird Cage was opened as a tourist attraction by the Hunley family, in whose hands it remains to this day.

With all of the authentic fixtures in place and the theatre's traumatic history, it is not surprising that this building is reputed to be the most haunted place in all of Tombstone. This is quite a claim in a town where ghosts are everywhere. In fact, the Bird Cage Theatre is the only building in the historic district that predates the terrible 1882 fire in Tombstone. This building and its ghosts are perhaps the toughest of all in Tombstone.

Sightings at the Bird Cage go back to the 1920s when a high school was built across the street from the old theatre. Students would vow they heard the sounds of singing from the Bird Cage. When the Bird Cage opened as a tourist attraction it was not long before everyone noticed that all was not quiet in this old theatre. Objects moved by themselves, loud voices and piano music were heard, and cloudy figures in old fashioned clothing flittered by. Over the years the stories have continued and to this day visitors report strange occurrences and all staff members seem to have had at least one ghostly experience.

One of the most common apparitions is a vaporous woman in white. I spoke with a staff member who spotted the women in white in 2005 near the birdcages, where visitors are not allowed. At first he thought it must be a tourist and he quickly went to tell her she was not allowed there. There was no one. Puzzled, he asked the other staff member who was in the theatre and she said no one had come into the place for the past hour. It is important to know there are cameras in all areas of the theatre that are monitored in the gift shop. There are also staff members at the entrance and exits to the theatre making it impossible for a visitor to arrive or leave without being seen.

Another day, this same staff member heard a woman's voice say, "Well, good morning," but when he turned to look, there was no one there. In fact the doors to the theatre were still locked and when he went to look outside to see if the voice had drifted in from the street, there was no one there either. A woman who worked at the Bird Cage Theatre several years ago also saw the woman in white in one of the hanging birdcages. She was alarmed as visitors are not allowed to go into the birdcages, and she thought she would lose her job, but when she approached the birdcage to tell the woman to leave, she had disappeared. This woman in white has been reported by many visitors and staff members over the years.

Another apparition often seen at the Bird Cage Theatre is a male spirit, who is seen walking across the stage. Sometimes he is just a dark shadow and other times he appears more clearly, walking from stage right to stage left in a pinstripe suit holding a clipboard. Is this a former stage manager eternally checking all the last minute details for the next performance?

The painting of Fatima in the lobby of the Bird Cage Theatre is reputed to be haunted. Many visitors have a surprise in their photographs of the painting. In some photos a skull will appear and in others a wolf. I was not successful in producing either image when I took my pictures, but copies of the photos other visitors have taken are at the bar. If you ask, you can see these strange photos with images of something that is not really there.

Night time is when the Bird Cage really comes alive. Employees do not like to be alone in the building after it closes. There's loud music when there is no band, voices speak from nowhere, laughter echoes, and the heavy scent of cigar smoke permeates the building. The old Wild West rough crowd arises to carouse as the theatre opens for the late night business again.

A staff member told me about a terrifying experience he had when he was at the bar giving his introductory speech to a group of tourists. Suddenly an unseen hand latched onto his left shoulder. It was like a bony vise grip as this otherworldly attacker caused so much pain, his arm was numb for two months. Just who attacked him is uncertain, but it might be the current owner's grandmother who bought the Bird Cage Theatre back in 1934. Perhaps she did not agree with the information he was giving in his talk, or just simply wanted to get this staff member's attention. Whatever her reasoning, the message was received, painfully and clearly.

Throughout the Bird Cage Theatre spirits abound. It is not that strange really, as twenty-six violent deaths occurred on the premises. Take note as you wander around the Bird Cage Theatre, you might catch the acrid smell of rotgut whiskey or cigar smoke, or you might hear echoes of ghostly laughter or singing. Perhaps you may even see the fading image of a man walking across the stage or a woman in white high up in one of the cribs. Try not to be alarmed, but revel in the fact that you have just been treated to a firsthand encounter with the illustrious past of the Bird Cage Theatre.

Of course the Bird Cage Theatre is not the only haunted place in Tombstone. Boothill Grave Yard is also the home to many spirits. Over two hundred and fifty graves are in Boothill today. For a small donation you can read a descriptive list of the graves, the names of the dead, and the cause of death, if known. Considering Tombstone's wild past, there are many grave markers stating death was by hanging, murder, or a mining injury. Billy Clanton, Tom McLaury, and Frank McLaury, who died as a result of the shoot-out at the OK Corral, are buried in Boothill cemetery. While the OK Corral itself seems as though it should be haunted, there are few stories of phantoms. Perhaps these outlaw spirits are trapped in the Boothill Grave Yard instead. Hiking the pathways in Boothill is like a history lesson of Tombstone. The graves are piled with stones and the head-markers all tell a sad story. There's a disquieting feeling to Boothill, of lives cut short, of violence and loss; a feeling of unquiet spirits who left things undone while they lived or who need to make atonement for foul deeds.

During my visit to Boothill, the staff in the Visitors'

Center all told me stories about ghostly experiences. One of the most common experiences in the Visitors' Center is books coming off display shelves. One time a staff member stated the books flew off the shelves so hard that it knocked her glasses off. Do these dead not like the way their exploits are retold in the books? Another employee commented that one day they all heard popcorn popping in the employee area but when they went back there, there was no popcorn, and no rational explanation for the sound. Was this, in fact, the faint muffled sounds of gunshots as the dead battled once again in the graveyard?

Just a few days prior to my visit in February 2007, one of the employees saw two visitors in the grave yard, a woman in a denim jacket and a man dressed in black. They wandered about without really looking at the graves, as if they saw something else in the dry dirt underfoot. This employee yelled out to them that it was closing time and went back into the visitor center. But these visitors never came back through the visitor center, which is the only real entrance and exit. When an employee went to look for them on the grounds they were not to be found.

In the past, there used to be a strong smell of cigar smoke, but it is not as prevalent anymore. Today, employees are treated to surprise ghostly visitors in the restroom as the door suddenly opens. Of course there is never anyone there to explain how the door opened; no one from this world anyway. Take note when you visit Boothill just who else is walking the graveyard with you; it just might be a spirit wandering the burial ground for eternity.

Another haunted location in Tombstone is Big Nose Kate's Saloon, which was originally the Grand Hotel and opened in September 1880. Many famous people in Tombstone's history stayed at the Grand Hotel, including Doc Holliday, the Earp brothers, the Clantons, and the McLaurys. In 1881 a huge fire tore through Allen Street in Tombstone, causing damage to countless buildings. It is believed that the charred remains of the Grand Hotel collapsed into the basement.

Before the fire swept through the Grand Hotel, local legend says that a building caretaker lived in the basement of the hotel. He spent a great deal of time in his room and dug a mineshaft down into the Toughnut Mine, where he was able to have access to large amounts of silver. What he did with this silver is unknown, but he has become known as "The Swamper". Today the entrance to this mineshaft can still be seen in the basement of Big Nose Kate's Saloon.

The Swamper is believed to be haunting the saloon, and

his presence can be felt in the basement and in the saloon itself. He is a cantankerous ghost. It is thought that he hid his silver in the hotel and he is spending his afterlife trying to protect it. The most common occurrences are hearing footsteps when no one is there, lights turning on and off by themselves, doors opening and closing, silverware thrown off the tables by unseen hands, and cases of beer falling over in the basement. It is also believed that the spirit of a cowboy haunts the bar, as photographs have been taken by visitors on several occasions in the bar only to have a cowboy appear in the developed image, when no one was there. If you're at the bar and hear boots on the floorboards coming up behind, along with the ring of spurs, be sure to order a second whiskey for the thirsty traveler from long ago.

Come to Tombstone and visit the historic Bird Cage Theatre, and see this legendary site for yourself. Wander the streets, mosey along the planked sidewalks under the weathered overhangs, and visit Boot Hill Cemetery where shadowy figures drift through the graveyard beside you. Perhaps you will stop for a drink at Big Nose Kate's Saloon where apparitions of cowboys are commonplace. Tombstone still shows tantalizing fragments of the Wild West days of Arizona. As a stagecoach thunders past you on Allen Street and shots ring out in a saloon, the days of tough gunfighters and miners and even tougher madams seem to come alive. This is a town the ghosts will not abandon.

16

Bisbee
These Inns were made for Haunting

Bisbee, Arizona strikes you as a fantasy after driving through the dark Mule Pass Tunnel and circling down the mountain into town. It is like a Victorian outpost nestled in this red soil hideaway of Arizona. Terraces of brightly painted houses and welcoming inns rise up from the town center. Picturesque streets packed with shops, stunning views from every corner, and the peaceful location make for a wonderful escape. Peaceful enough for ghosts too, because in Bisbee it seems every hotel and inn has resident spirits. So, when you rest your weary head at the end of the day, you might be surprised by a nighttime visitor drifting in from the hallway, coming to share your chamber.

Bisbee is a former copper mining town in the southeastern part of the state, close to the Mexico and New Mexico borders. In the early 1900s the Copper Queen Mine in Bisbee was the largest copper mine in the world and the population in town soared to twenty thousand people. By 1950 the population of Bisbee had dropped to around six thousand people. Because strip mining continued for many years, this town did not suffer the fate of most other mining towns and disappear. In 1975 the Phelps Dodge Corporation finally closed the mine. Like Jerome, Arizona, artists adopted Bisbee as a place to live, and tourism grew in the area as well.

The town is nestled in the Mule Gulch of the Mule Mountains. (A gulch is a v-shaped depression caused by erosion.) Bisbee was first settled in 1880 when rich copper deposits were discovered in the Mule Mountains. Bisbee was named for Judge DeWitt Bisbee, a financier of the Copper Queen Mine. This mine ultimately became one of the richest mineral deposits in the world. Over the years, the mine produced almost 3 million ounces of gold, over 8 billion pounds of copper, 97 million ounces of silver, 304 million pounds of lead, and 273 million pounds of zinc deposits.

Because Bisbee is located in a gulch, formed from two canyons (Tombstone Canyon and Brewery Gulch), the town is very hilly, with homes perched on cliff sides, often overlooking their neighbor's backyards. Through the years Bisbee suffered through several disasters including floods and fires, along with typhoid, smallpox, and diphtheria outbreaks. These caused many deaths and may account for the haunted feel to the whole town. As you walk along the twisting streets and alleys, there is a forlorn sense, a feeling of loss even with all the bright facades. Despite the disasters the mines continued to operate around the clock, and the citizens of Bisbee recovered and re-built, determined to stay in their town. Their efforts can be seen today as Bisbee retains many historic buildings and inns. But there are also remnants of the natural disasters seen in tottering old cabins, stairs that lead to nowhere, and the ruins of old buildings. The cemeteries retell the grim fates of those who died.

Ruins of old Bisbee

Perhaps not all of the dead have truly passed. Myranda Symons, an employee at the Bisbee Grand Hotel, recounted an episode at a cemetery. The night before a wedding, she and three friends ventured into the Bisbee cemetery on a lark for a thrill with the dead. Laughing they raced deep into the graveyard. In the dark quiet every little puff of wind or soft unknown scratching was amplified and struck them cold, a little afraid, but still giddy and excited. They stopped to enjoy the uncanny atmosphere. Gray tombstones, broken crosses and leaning pillars seemed to glow as they stretched away into the blackness. One of her female friends reached out to touch an old crumbling gravestone, partly hidden by overgrowth. Straight away, she yanked her hand away and stammered, "So cold." She stumbled; she had a strange silver dullness in her eyes as if catatonic; then she fainted. They all just stared at her a moment as she lay pale and still on the dark grass. Something seemed to rustle by the gravestone. Quickly, a male friend picked her up and they all ran for the gates. This was no longer fun. Myranda felt they were being pursued and looking back she saw the grass depress here and there as if by feet. Screaming, she ran even faster. Trying to catch up to her friends she kept hearing steps chasing on the gravel road. The gates were near and her friends were going out. The footfalls were right behind her now. Just at the gates something pushed her, causing Myranda to trip and fall outside the cemetery. Was it real or did she imagine a horrid low moaning? She got to her feet and they just kept running after that.

After these terrifying events, the group went to the Copper Queen Hotel to recover. Myranda nestled into a big chair in the lobby to rest her aching ankle, which she had twisted in her fall at the cemetery gates. All of a sudden, she felt smothered, as if someone was on top of her, pressing her down into the chair. It was terrifying; she could not breathe but chocked and struggled. Thankfully, one of her friends saw something was wrong and yanked Myranda off the chair. This was too much for one night and Myranda fell into the arms of her friend. Apparently the chair is the favorite haunt of a spirit. A gentleman ghost, complete with a top hat, is supposed to sit in the chair; perhaps he does not like to share his resting space with others.

The Bisbee Grand Hotel, built in 1906, was used mostly as accommodations for executives who were visiting the Copper Queen Mines. The hotel sits on a curve in Main Street, near antique shops, artist's shops, and is a short walk to the Bisbee Mining Museum. With only two stories, the hotel is quiet and intimate; but this is during the day. There are seven uniquely themed suites, six comfortable rooms, and a full service saloon. Besides having unique and historic accommodations the Bisbee Grand Hotel has other amenities as well: it has ghosts.

The most commonly seen ghost is called the "Victorian Woman" who is dressed in red, with a red bonnet. She is described as being thirty to forty years old, about 5'5" tall with long blond hair, cascading down her back. She is believed to have been a prostitute and is most often seen in or around the Victorian Suite (which is right above the lobby of the hotel). While working in the lobby, staff have heard the Victorian Lady walking around upstairs when no one is in the room. Several people have seen her, including Myranda Symons, who as noted earlier is an employee at the Bisbee Grand Hotel. Myranda was upstairs cleaning one day, when she saw the Victorian Woman out of the corner of her eye. She describes this as a passing glimpse, as if the Victorian Woman wants people to know that she is there, but not to get too close to her. Who exactly this person was or why she haunts the Bisbee Grand Hotel remains unknown.

Another ghost at the Bisbee Grand Hotel makes his presence known in the lobby by whispering indistinctly to the staff. His words are muffled as if he is purposely hiding his meaning or perhaps he is struggling to say something but is unable to do so from beyond. Myranda confirms that she has heard this man, whom she thinks is in his thirties or forties from the sound of his voice murmuring to her, but does not know what he is saying.

The third ghost haunting the Bisbee Grand Hotel is a little boy. He has been seen and heard throughout the hotel. He plays happily, running up and down the stairs. He has been known to take people's belongings, only to return them later. Visitors traveling with children sometimes hear their toys played with during the night. Determined to scold their children for being up in the middle of the night, these parents are shocked to find their children sound asleep, and no visible source for the joyful playing they had heard moments before. The most haunted locations in the hotel appear to be the lobby, the Victorian Room, and the Captain's Suite, although odd events have been known to occur throughout the hotel.

During our stay in Bisbee, we stayed in the Captain's Suite of the Bisbee Grand Hotel, which is a series of rooms including two large bedrooms and a large sitting room. I was delighted at how spacious the rooms were and chose the Captain's Room for my son's nap. I set up everything as always on trips and put him down for a rest. When I closed the door, he started crying immediately. He did not stop, but became louder and began to scream. Opening the door I found him, standing, shivering, and clutching his blanket, crying uncontrollably. Thinking his nap schedule was off, we took him for a walk and he finally fell asleep in his stroller. That night, I prepared my son for bed and everything seemed fine, but the moment I set him in his bed, he panicked, screamed, and cried. He wanted out of the room. He seemed okay in the front sitting room. Believing the Captain's Room was scaring him (there is a rather odd and scary picture of an old Sea Whaler on the wall) we tried putting him in the front bedroom, called the Crew's Quarters. He cried again. Trying to calm him down I attempted to set up a portable DVD player, which we had used during the drive down from Phoenix. The DVD player had sound, but no picture. (The next day in the car the DVD worked fine without adjusting anything.) We finally had to take him for a drive to calm him down and get him to fall asleep. However, he was never happy in any of the bedrooms that night and was only calm when we were in the sitting room. Could he sense the ghostly activity in the bedrooms?

During the night, my father, who was traveling with me, along with my mother, had a strange experience in the Captain's Room. He is a researcher and planner, who wants evidence, and is not prone to frights. Just before retiring, he put back the gloomy picture, which we had turned against the wall because of the brooding dark eyes that always seemed to have just turned away from looking at you. Even the face of the Whaler was off, fishlike with bulging lips and neck folds like gills. During the night he heard a sharp knock or bell from a long distance, but also loud and dangerous. Then there was a rush of cool air as if a door had opened. He felt the suite was threatened by someone and he was going to rise to check the other rooms. Then he felt a huge weight upon him, holding down his arms, crushing him into the bed. Struggling he tried to lift his arms and could not; he was paralyzed. There was an overpowering feeling of danger, as if a malignant force was upon him. Thrashing about again and again he finally threw off the thing. At last he woke into the darkness of the chamber. The thing was gone and the suite was quiet and peaceful. My mother told me later that she was startled awake by my father's struggling.

The Bisbee Grand Hotel is not the only haunted hotel in Bisbee. The Copper Queen Hotel is also reputed to be haunted. The Copper Queen Hotel was constructed in 1902 by the Copper Queen Mining Company.

Like the Bisbee Grand Hotel, the Copper Queen has three resident ghosts, a woman, a man and a young boy; another family of ghosts. Myranda Symons' experiences with the gentleman ghost at the Copper Queen Hotel have already been explored. The woman is the most famous eerie presence in the hotel. She was a prostitute, Julia Lowell, who fell in love with one of her clients. When her love was not returned she killed herself at the hotel. Her hotel room, Room 315, is still haunted, as is the entire third floor of the hotel. Julia has been known to whisper into ears of guests, dance at the foot of the bed, pull the blankets off the bed, and tickle men's feet staying in her room. During an episode of Ghost Hunters on the Sci-Fi Channel, there was some dramatic footage of Julia's antics. As one of the members of the team, Grant, was sleeping in his room, the covers were pulled off the bed. This was captured on camera, and there appeared to be no rational explanation for how this could have happened. While the Ghost Hunters did not feel they could decisively conclude that this was the result of ghostly activity, the staff at the Copper Queen Hotel knew Julia was at work.

The little boy haunts the fourth floor of the hotel, moving guests' belongings around. The boy, who is known as Billy, is believed to have drowned in the San Pedro River (which runs from Mexico about seventeen miles west of Bisbee). He is particularly fascinated with televisions and enjoys turning them on and off, changing the channels, or just making them impossible to work. In the hotel, he is always discovering new toys to play with during the night. And you may hear the patter of little feet as he sprints away with a new find. Yet he seems to be a well-behaved, caring boy for he returns the playthings, but not always to the same spot.

Another haunted inn in Bisbee is the Hotel La More (also known as the Bisbee Inn) located above Historic Brewery Gulch. The Hotel La More was built in 1916 by Mrs. S.P. Bedford, and opened in 1917 by Mrs. Kate La More. The location was convenient to the mine and also to the saloons and prostitute cribs in Brewery Gulch. The inn changed hands over the years being converted into an apartment building in the 1940s and a volunteer training center in the 1960s. In 1982 the house was restored and converted back into an historic hotel. The ghost that haunts this hotel is a lady dressed in white, who brings a sweet scent of lilacs. She has been seen throughout the hotel and sometimes a ghost cat has been reported in Room 23. If you decide to make the Hotel La More a part of your stay in Bisbee do not be surprised if your bed is turned down, or furniture rearranged, or if you are suddenly overcome with the perfume of lilacs. It is simply the woman in white wandering the hotel and making sure you are comfortable, always bearing a delicate, sweet floral fragrance along the hallways and into the rooms.

The Oliver House Bed and Breakfast is another haunted inn in Bisbee. This bed and breakfast was built in 1909 by Edith Ann Oliver. It was originally built as offices for the mine, before becoming a boarding house, and finally converted into a Bed and Breakfast. This house has a violent history with a reported twenty-seven deaths and five ghosts haunting the home. Room 13 is the most haunted, and the activity in this room can possibly be traced to the murder of Nat Anderson, who was killed just outside of this room on February 22, 1920. Some people also say that the wife of a local police officer was having an affair with a man in the Oliver House; when her husband found them, he killed them both and then committed suicide.

In the Grandma Room, an elderly lady died of old age, but her spirit has not left the house. She still rocks in her favorite rocking chair, sometimes moving it closer to the window to enjoy the view. She occasionally dusts the room in which she has chosen to spend eternity. Throughout this old inn, houseguests have heard unexplained footsteps, windows and doors open and close, and experienced sudden unexplained cold spots. A stay at the Oliver House Bed and Breakfast is sure to be a pleasure with some possible unexpected thrills.

The Inn at Castle Rock in Bisbee, built in 1899, is also haunted. Like many of the other haunted inns in this town, the Inn at Castle Rock started as a miners' boarding house. It was later converted to apartments and was opened as an inn in 1982. The inn is directly across from Castle Rock on Tombstone Canyon and is the largest wood building in Old Bisbee. It was built in the Queen Anne style, with wraparound porches, and is also known as the Muirhead House as it was constructed by John Muirhead, the first mayor of Bisbee. The hotel is unique because it is situated on the location of the US Cavalry encampment in 1877 and also on top of a spring used by the first settlers in Bisbee. Those staying in the Inn at Castle Rock are truly staying in the origins of Old Bisbee, and can see the spring, which helped those first settlers survive the often-harsh Arizona conditions. Today this spring is a fishpond with Japanese Koi making it their home.

Visitors to the Inn at Castle Rock might also get to view history firsthand. The spirit of an old miner has been seen in the inn, especially in the Return to Paradise Room. The spirit of a woman dressed in Victorian clothing has been seen on the stairs. Whoever these spirits really are haunting the Inn at Castle Rock, they seem content and mostly only show themselves in a shadowy form. If the Inn at Castle Rock is where you choose to stay during your time at Bisbee, you just might experience one of these spirits, and if not, you will still enjoy the notable hotel built on a very historic location.

While speaking with locals in Bisbee I was told that almost everything in this town was haunted. With the number of stories from the inns this certainly rings true. If you choose to vacation in Bisbee the historic feel of the town will charm you. Be sure to visit the Copper Queen Mine, which is open for tours, and has rumors of being haunted itself. If you spend the night, choose one of the many historic haunted hotels in town. There are many spirits in this old Arizona mining town, some friendly and comforting, others scary and threatening. Remember you have journeyed into their eternal homes and always make room for them in your hotel or inn.

Fairbank Ghost Town

empty rooms and landscape. Here ghosts roam and enjoy their former homes, or relive over and over again their tragic deaths. These are Arizona's ghost towns.

Arizona has hundreds of abandoned ghost towns scattered throughout the state. Some have several large impressive crumbling buildings and some have a few sparse ruins, or simply an abandoned mine shaft as a sign of former glory. Some of these towns can be quite a challenge to locate and require some careful navigating. Four towns in particular are called "ghost towns" for reason other than just the fact they are abandoned - Fairbank, Gleeson, Courtland and the bloodiest cabin in Arizona history, Brunckow's cabin.

Fairbank lies only ten miles west of Tombstone and its life began in 1881 when a railroad depot was created there. Eventually Fairbank would serve three rail lines, as a stopping point from Benson to Nogales, Tombstone, and Bisbee. In 1882 Tombstone boasted a population of 15,000 people and Fairbank became the main supply depot for this Wild West town. Fairbank itself only ever had a population of one hundred people, but because of its large depots it had a number of substantial buildings including restaurants, saloons, a hotel, and a jail. Today the town of Fairbank is part of the San Pedro Riparian National Conservation Area, and visitors can pick up a brochure to take a self guided tour around the town. Several buildings still stand including a large commercial building from 1883 that held the general store, post office, and a saloon. The foundations of the Montezuma hotel remain near the commercial building.

A small house built in 1885 remains, as does a 1925 house, and a 1920 school house. The commercial building is now surrounded by a chain link fence and the building is stabilized by large wooden beams. You cannot enter the buildings at this time. Despite that, the remains are impressive and give a sense of a lost community. As a strange counter to the abandoned and desolated feeling that emanates from the buildings, there are picnic tables for visitors to this ghost town.

Fairbank cemetery

Since Fairbank is on Highway 82 on the way to Tombstone, it is an easy ghost town to visit, with no need to go long distances on gravel roads, or walk through the brush. This results in a number of visitors, and on our visit on a cold, windy and rainy day in February several other groups were exploring the town. To get a real sense of the desolation and feel the echoes of the ghosts, a visit to the Fairbank cemetery is a must. The cemetery is about a half mile walk from the main ruin site and is a true ghost town cemetery. Here the grave markers tumble down and stand at sharp angles. Old cast iron fences rust away and bricks lie in tumbled piles. Here you can feel the ghosts of Fairbank residents who toiled for hours loading and unloading the rail cars or working long thankless hours in the saloons and stores. Here you can feel the life of this small town that lived for such a short period of time before fading away in the 1930s.

Heading east from Tombstone for fifteen miles on Gleeson Road, you will find the ghost town of Gleeson. This fifteen mile drive will take an hour as the washboard gravel road has you driving as slowly as five miles an hour at times. Only a few travelers make the journey. All around us as we drove to Gleeson were dark clouds swirling, and as we finally approached Gleeson, which can be seen by the ruins on either side of the road, it began to snow. Although Gleeson is supposed to have a few inhabitants I did not see any among the abandoned buildings. The only sign of life was a dog that came bounding along the road, barking furiously as I ran back to the car. Was he on guard for the ruined buildings, making sure visitors did not take anything away? Or perhaps he was warning me that there are otherworldly presences in this ghost town, and I should leave at once, lest I encounter them as well.

Gleeson began its life as the camp of Turquoise, where for years local Native Americans mined the precious stone. Turquoise began as a mining town in 1890, but the post office closed down in 1894. John Gleeson, a miner working in Pearce, discovered copper near Turquoise. The camp was moved downhill to be closer to the water supply and renamed Gleeson. The new Gleeson post office opened on Oct. 15, 1900. By 1909 the town had swelled to five hundred people and there were several large buildings, including a school, a hospital and a jail. In 1912 a horrible fire devastated much of Gleeson, destroying twenty-eight buildings. The town rebuilt, and the demand for copper during the First World War helped to boost its economy. But as with all mining towns, the copper veins eventually played out, the occupants left, and on March 31, 1939 the post office

207

closed. Despite being a virtual ghost town for almost seventy years, a few hardy occupants apparently still live in Gleeson. It is hard to imagine what they do here along this lonely stretch of road so far away from civilization, but perhaps they have found peace in the quiet hills and memories of the past. As you see the crumbling ruins, and the shells of once grand buildings, you can faintly hear the echoes of the former miners in this town. The foundations of the buildings and hollow shells still smell faintly from the fires that frequently ravaged this town, and ghosts still wander the fields and gravel roads of Gleeson.

Leaving Gleeson and taking the Ghost Town Trail north six miles you will arrive in Courtland. Like Gleeson Road this gravel road is bumpy and rough, and the short distance takes twenty-five minutes to navigate through. Today Courtland is completely abandoned, a true ghost town, with no brochures or parking lots to greet would be tourists. Instead all you will find are the ruins of the jail, a collapsing store, several foundations, and hills pocketed with mines and shafts making hiking in the area a perilous affair.

Courtland's post office opened in 1909, and several mining companies operated here including the Copper Queen, Great Western, Calumet and Arizona. The town's population grew to two thousand people, and several large buildings were built, including a large jail. Recreational activities were also established with an ice cream parlor, a swimming pool, and a movie theater in town. The town had two newspapers, and a railroad served the area from Douglas, Arizona.

Like Gleeson, the mines in Courtland played out and closed for good in the 1940s, with the post office closing in 1942. By this time many of the buildings had already been demolished, or moved, and the few crumbling ruins were left to melt in the Arizona desert. While no humans call Courtland home, who knows what spirits remain.

The last ghost town remnant that will be visited in this chapter is Brunckow's Cabin, the bloodiest cabin in Arizona history. As there is much confusion over the location of the cabin, and several people (myself included on my first visit) are mistaking another set of ruins for the cabin, I will give specific directions on finding the cabin. Leaving Tombstone, travel west on the Charleston Road (called Sumner St. in Tombstone) for just under eight miles until you see a red street sign on the left (south) side of the road for Brunckow Road. Turning in at this gravel road you see a gravel parking space immediately on your right. You must park here, as no cars are allowed down the road as this is part of the San Pedro Riparian National Conservation Area. Walk south down this gravel road for about fifty feet and you will come upon a small set of adobe ruins. This low set of ruins, crumbling and melting into the desert is believed by many to be Brunckow's Cabin, but it is not. Turn right and head west, you will pass a set of concrete ruins as well, but stay on the trail and keep walking. If you have binoculars with you, you can see the ruins of Brunckow's Cabin from this point, set up on a small hill directly west with the mountains beyond it. Keep walking along this trail for about a half mile and it will take you down a small hill into a wash and then up onto the small hill where Brunckow's Cabin stands today. There is a small sign in front of the cabin, not stating what the ruins are, but that they are part of the San Pedro Riparian National Conservation Area, and that visitors can not take any artifacts with them and there is no shooting in the area. This last regulation is apparently taken lightly, as the path to the cabin, and the area around it, is surrounded with numerous spent bullet casings.

Also surrounding the cabin are the rusted and decayed remains of old tin cans and canteens. Just a short walk north of the cabin down a small hill there is a large congregation of these old metal remains, several of which are now riddled with bullet holes. This area looks like it was the trash pit for the mine. Interestingly there is little evidence of fires or beer bottles around this site (which are found in abundance at the first set of ruins nearer the road), perhaps because many people never make it to the true ruins.

Brunckow's Cabin has a bloody history and a long association with ghosts. The cabin was built in 1858 by Frederick Brunckow who worked on some mining claims nearby. Evidence of former mining efforts can be seen all around the cabin. The cabin itself is one room with a large fireplace in the corner. The exterior of the walls are adobe, while the interior is concrete. Seeing photographs of Brunckow's Cabin in Thelma Heatwole's *Ghost Towns and Historical Haunts in Arizona*, it is startling to see how much damage has occurred to the cabin in the last fifty years, and at this rate it seems only foundations will remain fifty years from now.

What of the stories that this is the bloodiest cabin in Arizona's history? The stories began early in the cabin's history when several violent deaths occurred. Living with Brunckow were John Moss the assayer, the cook David Brontrager, James Williams the machinist, and William Williams the mine superintendent. On a Monday morning in 1860 William Williams made the long forty mile journey to Fort Buchanan to obtain supplies. He returned to the camp four days later on July 26th and discovered a bloody scene. The first thing he noticed was the silence, then on entering the cabin he found Moss and Williams, dead. Brunckow was found dead supposedly with a rock drill through him, his body dumped down the mine shaft.

Williams fled the bloody mess. Several days later Brontrager was found, he said that the Mexican laborers had attacked shortly after Williams had left, and had taken everything of value with them.

In 1874 bloodshed occurred yet again at Brunckow's cabin. Arizona's first U.S. marshal, Major Milton B. Duffield, arrived at Brunckow's cabin stating he owned the mine. James T. Holmes, who lived in the cabin, also claimed he owned the mine, and holding his shotgun declared that if Duffield came any closer he would shoot. Duffield ignored the warning, and Holmes shot him in the head. By the 1880s it was said that at least twenty men had lost their lives in the cabin, giving it the legend of being cursed.

Not all associations with the cabin are negative. It is said Ed Schieffelin used the fireplace at Brunckow's Cabin in 1877 to assay (determine the quality and quantity of the ore) the samples that led to his series of successful mines around Tombstone.

But despite this one positive association, the cabin has long been known as the bloodiest in Arizona's history, and ghosts have long been suspected of inhabiting the cabin. On May 20, 1891 an article in the Arizona Democrat stated about Brunckow's Cabin, "Many will tell you that the unquiet spirits of the departed ones are wont to revisit the glimpses of the moon and wander about the scene which witnesses their untimely taking off. The graves lie thick about the place." Even today those who manage to find the cabin, and are brave enough to visit it at night, report visions of spirits fleeting around the cabin and down the abandoned mine shafts. It is not surprising that such lonesome spirits should congregate here, the scene where they all met their bloody ends. It would take a brave person indeed to spend the night with these souls, hearing the shrieks and feeling their fear. As for me, during my daytime visit, I was struck by the silence of the place, the stillness, eerie in itself, the littered remains of the former occupants, and bullet casings, a memento of a violent past. Standing in the cabin I could faintly hear voices echoing off the walls, and the cries from beyond sent the faintest chill down my spine.

A visit to the historic haunts of Arizona is not complete without a visit to a true ghost town, so after your visit to Tombstone, take in the local ghostly haunts of Fairbank, Gleeson, and Courtland along the ghost town trail. But remember that no visit to Arizona would be complete without viewing the bloodiest cabin of all, Brunckow's Cabin, standing alone on its hill, a reminder of the bloody, violent past in this area. Here you will sense the spirits and ghosts of Arizona's haunted history.

Appendix 1
Location Directory

Please contact sites for hours of operation and current admission fees.

Bird Cage Theatre
517 E. Allen St.
Tombstone, AZ 85638
800-457-3423
www.tombstoneaz.net
oldbirdcage@juno.com

Bisbee Grand Hotel
61 Main Street
Bisbee, AZ 85603
520-432-5900
www.bisbeegrandhotel.com
BisBeeGrand@CableOne.net

Casey Moore's Oyster House
850 S. Ash Avenue
Tempe, AZ 85281
480-968-9935
www.myspace.com/caseymoores

Copper Queen Hotel
11 Howell Avenue
Bisbee, AZ 85603
520-432-2216
www.copperqueen.com
info@copperqueen.com

Courtland Ghost Town
www.ghosttowns.com/states/az/courtland.html

El Tovar Hotel
C/O Xanterra South Rim, L.L.C.
P.O. Box 699
Grand Canyon, AZ 86023
928-638-2631
www.grandcanyonlodges.com/el-tovar-409.html

Fairbank Ghost Town
www.ghosttowns.com/states/az/fairbank.html

Gammons Gulch Old West Town
PO Box 76
Pomerene, AZ. 85627
520-212-2831
www.gammonsgulch.com
gammonsgulch@gammonsgulch.com

Gleeson Ghost Town
www.ghosttowns.com/states/az/gleeson.html

Gold King Mine & Ghost Town
P.O. Box 125
Jerome, AZ 86331
928-634-0053
www.goldkingmineghosttown.com

Grand Canyon National Park
P.O. Box 129
Grand Canyon, AZ 86023
928-638-7888
www.nps.gov/grca

Haunted Hamburger
Jerome Avenue
Jerome, AZ 86331
928-634-0554
www.jeromechamber.com/pages/dining

Hotel La More ~ The Bisbee Inn
45 Oak Street
Bisbee, AA 85603
520-432-5131
www.hotellamore.com

Hotel Monte Vista
100 N. San Francisco St.
Flagstaff, AZ 86001
928-779-6971
www.hotelmontevista.com

Hotel San Carlos
202 North Central Avenue
Phoenix, AZ 85004
602-253-4121
www.hotelsancarlos.com

Hotel Vendome
230 South Cortez Street
Prescott, AZ 86303
928-776-0900
www.vendomehotel.com
vendomehotel@aol.com

The Inn at Castle Rock
112 Tombstone Canyon Rd.
Bisbee, AZ 85603
520-432-7868

Jerome Grand Hotel
200 Hill Street
Jerome, AZ
928-634-8200
www.jeromegrandhotel.net

Jerome Historical Society
407 Clark Street
Jerome, AZ 86331
www.jeromehistoricalsociety.org

Landmark Restaurant
809 W. Main Street
Mesa, AZ 85201
480-962-4652
www.lmrk.com

Monti's
100 S. Mill Avenue
Tempe, AZ 85281
480-967-7594
www.montis.com

Oliver House Bed and Breakfast
26 Sowles Road
Bisbee, AZ 85603
520-432-1900
oliverhouse@theriver.com

Orpheum Theatre
15 W. Aspen Street
Flagstaff, AZ 86001
928-556-1580
www.orpheumpresents.com

Prescott Fine Arts Association
208 N. Marina Street
Prescott, AZ 86301
928-445-3286
www.pfaa.net

The Red Garter Inn & Bakery
137 Railroad Avenue
Williams, AZ 86046
(928) 635-1484 | (800) 328-1484
www.redgarter.com
info@redgarter.com

Riordan Mansion State Historic Park
409 West Riordan Road
Flagstaff, AZ 86001
(928) 779-4395
www.azparks.gov/Parks/parkhtml/riordan.html

Teeter House
622 East Adams
Phoenix, AZ 85004
602-252-4682
www.theteeterhousecom

Tumacácori National Historical Park
1891 East Frontage Road
Tumacácori, AZ 85640
520-398-2341
www.nps.gov/tuma/

Verkamp's Curios
P.O. Box 96
Grand Canyon, AZ 86023
928-638-2242
www.verkamps.com
info@verkamps.com

Vulture Mine
36610 North 335 Ave.
Wickenburg, AZ 85390
602-859-2743
www.jpc-training.com/vulture.htm

Weatherford Hotel
23 N. Leroux
Flagstaff, AZ 86001
928-779-1919
www.weatherfordhotel.com
information@weatherfordhotel.com

Yuma Territorial Prison State Historic Park
1 Prison Hill Road
Yuma, AZ 85364
(928) 783-4771
www.azparks.gov/Parks/parkhtml/yuma.html

Appendix 2
Ghost Tours in Arizona

Most ghost tours are seasonal and require reservations. Please call ahead before visiting.

Bisbee
Old Bisbee Ghost Tour
520-432-3308
www.oldbisbeeghosttour.com

Jerome
Annual Ghost Walk
928-634-1066
www.jeromehistoricalsociety.org

Flagstaff
Riordan Mansion Annual Ghost Tours
(928) 779-4395
www.azparks.gov/Parks/parkhtml/riordan.html

Phoenix
Ghosts of Phoenix Tour
602-414-0004
www.ghostsofphoenix.com

Prescott
Sharlot Hall Museum Annual Ghost Walk
928-445-3122
www.sharlot.org

Tombstone
Tombstone Ghosts & Legends Tours
520-457-9400
www.tombstoneghostsandlegends.com

Tombstone Ghost Tour
520-432-3308
Tombstoneghosttour.com

Friends of the Dead
Tombstone Spirit Tours
 520 457-9191 ~ 1-866-311-9191
www.tombstoneweb.com/attractions.html

Tucson
Lost Souls Ghost Tours
61 East Congress St.
520-795-1117
lostsoulsparanormalinvestigations.com/ghostours.html

Tumacacori
Full Moon Tours
520-398-2341
www.nps.gov/tuma/

Williams
Saloon Row Ghost Tour
928-706-0703
www.saloonrowtour.com

Yuma
Yuma Ghost tour
928-446-5167
www.spirithunter.net/ghost_hunter_tours.htm

Bibliography

Anderson, Dorothy Daniels. *Arizona Legends and Lore: Tales of Southwestern Pioneers.* Phoenix: Golden West Publishers, 2005.

Armstrong, William Patrick. *Fred Harvey: Creator of Western Hospitality.* Bellemont, AZ: Canyonlands Publications, 2000.

Asfar, Dan. *Ghost Stories of Arizona and New Mexico.* Auburn, WA: Lone Pine Publishing International, 2006.

____. *Ghost Stories of the Old West.* Auburn, WA: Ghost House Books, 2003.

Barnes, Christine. *El Tovar: Celebrating 100 Years.* Bend, OR: W.W.West, Inc., 2001.

Berke, Arnold. *Mary Colter: Architect of the Southwest.* New York: Princeton Architectural Press, 2002.

Branning, Debe. *Sleeping With Ghosts! A Ghost Hunter's Guide to Arizona's Haunted Hotels and Inns.* Phoenix: Golden West Publishers, 2004.

Coulombe, Charles A. *Haunted Places in America: A Guide to Spooked and Spooky Public Places in the United States.* Guilford, CT: The Lyones Press, 2004.

Edwards, Ken. *Hotel Vendome: The Story of Prescott's Historic 1917 Hotel,* 2006.

____. *In Search of Abby: The Story of Prescott's Famous Ghost*. Np, nd.

Eppinga, Jane. *Arizona Twilight Tales: Good Ghosts, Evil Spirits and Blue Ladies*. Boulder, CO: Pruett Publishing Company, 2000.

Evans, Edna. *Tales from the Grand Canyon: Some True, Some Tall*. Flagstaff, AZ: Northland Press, 1976

Farretta, Kathy and Nikki Lober. *Community Builders: the Riordan Families of Flagstaff*. Arizona State Parks, 2006.

Garcez, Antonio, R. *American Indian Ghost Stories of the Southwest*. Truth or Consequences, NM: Red Rabbit Press, 2000.

____. *Arizona Ghost Stories*. Hanover, NM: Red Rabbit Press, 2003.

Harvey, Joe and Susie. *Ghost Stories From Tombstone Arizona*. Np, 2006

Hauck, Dennis William. *Haunted Places: The National Directory*. New York: Penguin Books, 2002.

Heatwole, Thelma. *Ghost Towns and Historical Haunts in Arizona*. Phoenix: Golden West Publishers, 1991.

Kermeen, Frances. *Ghostly Encounters: True Stories of American's Haunted Inns and Hotels*. New York: Warner Books, 2002.

Kiefer, D. R. *Haunts of Arizona*. Mesa, AZ: Shadow Publishings, 2000.

Knotts, Richard. *Riordan Mansion: Arizona's Arts & Crafts Treasure*. Phoenix: Arizona State Parks, 2002.

Lankford, Andrea. *Haunted Hikes: Spine-Tingling Tales and Trails from North America's National Parks*. Santa Monica, CA: Santa Monica Press LLC, 2006.

Lubick, George. *Petrified Forest National Park: A Wilderness Bound in Time*. Tucson: The University of Arizona Press, 1996.

McAlester, Virginia and Lee. *A Field Guide to American Houses*. New York: Alfred A. Knopf, 2000.

Miller, Donald C. *Ghost Towns of the Southwest*. Boulder, CO: Pruett Publishing Company, 1980.

Murbarger, Nell. *Ghosts of the Adobe Walls: Human Interest and Historical Highlights from 400 Arizona Ghost Haunts*. Los Angeles: Westernlore Press, 1964.

Murray, Earl. *Ghosts of the Old West*. New York: A Tor Book, 1988.

Noble, David Grant. *Ancient Ruins of the Southwest: An Archaeological Guide, 2nd Ed*. Flagstaff, AZ: Northland Publishing, 2000.

Norman, Michael and Beth Scott. *Haunted America*. New York: A Tor Book, 1994.

____. *Haunted Heritage*. New York: A Forge Book, 2002.

____. *Historic Haunted America*. New York: A Tor Book, 1995.

Petrillo, Alan M. "Spirits in Centennial Hall." The *University of Arizona Alumnus* (Fall 2006): 56-58.

Pyne, Stephen J. *How the Canyon Became Grand: A Short History*. New York: Penguin Books, 1999.

Robson, Ellen. *Haunted Arizona: Ghosts of the Grand Canyon State*. Phoenix: Golden West Publishers, 2004.

Robson, Ellen and Dianne Halicki. *Haunted Highway: The Spirits of Route 66*. Phoenix: Golden West Publisher, 2004.

Ryan, Pat M. "Tombsone Theatre Tonight!" *The Smoke Signal* Spring 1966.

Sammons, Mary Beth and Robert Edwards. *City Ghosts: True Tales of Hauntings in America's Cities*. New York: Sterling Publishing, 2006.

____. *American Hauntings*. New York: Barnes and Noble Publishing, 2005.

Shelton, Richard. *Going Back to Bisbee*. Tucson: The University of Arizona Press, 1992.

Sherman, James E. and Barbara H. *Ghost Towns of Arizona*. Norman, OK: University of Oklahoma Press, 1969.

Smith, Barbara. *Haunted Theaters*. Edmonton, AB: Ghost House Books, 2002.

Stampoulos, Linda L. *Visiting the Grand Canyon: Views of Early Tourism*. Charleston, SC: Arcadia Publishing, 2004.

Steiger, Brad. *Real Ghosts, Restless Spirits, and Haunted Places*. Canton, MI: Visible Ink Press, 2003.

Thybony, Scott. *The Incredible Grand Canyon: Cliffhangers and Curiosities From America's Greatest Canyon*. Grand Canyon, AZ: Grand Canyon Association, 2007.

Traywick, Ben T. *Ghost Towns & Lost Treasures*. Tombstone, AZ: Red Marie's Bookstore, 1994.

____. *The Chronicles of Tombstone*. Tombstone, AZ: Red Marie's Bookstore, 1994.

Trimble, Marshall. *Roadside History of Arizona*. Missoula, MT: Mountain Press Publishing Co., 2004. 2nd Ed.

Varney, Philip. *Arizona Ghost Towns and Mining Camps: A Travel Guide to History*. Phoenix: Arizona Highways, 2006.

Wildfang, Frederic B., and Sharlot Hall Museum Archives. *Images of America: Prescott*. Charleston, SC: Arcadia Publishing, 2006.

Young, Gloria. *The Ghost Trackers Guide to Haunted Tombstone*. Instant Publisher, Inc., 2004.

Index

About the Author

Jill Pascoe is a native of Winnipeg, Manitoba, Canada. She has a B.A. in Archaeology and History from McGill University and a M.A. in Museum Studies from University College London. She has worked at historic houses and museums in Canada, England, New Jersey, and Virginia. This is her second book. Her first book, *Louisiana's Haunted Plantations* was published in 2004.

Jill lives in Gilbert, Arizona with her husband Josh, their son Adam, and their cats Lancelot, Guinevere and Tessa. She enjoys spending time with her son, reading, writing, and exploring haunted locations around the world.

If you have a ghost story to share from any part of the globe please send it to: stories@irongatepress.com.